Analyzing Library Collection Use with Excel®

Tony Greiner and Bob Cooper

AMERICAN LIBRARY ASSOCIATION
Chicago   2007

Design and composition by ALA Editions in Minion and Futura using InDesign 2.0 for the PC

The paper used in this publication meets the minimum requirements of American National Standard for Information Sciences—Permanence of Paper for Printed Library Materials, ANSI Z39.48-1992. ∞

Library of Congress Cataloging-in-Publication Data

Greiner, Tony.
    Analyzing library collection use with Excel / Tony Greiner and Bob Cooper.
       p.   cm.
    Includes bibliographical references and index.
    ISBN 0-8389-0933-7 (alk. paper)
    1. Library use studies. 2. Microsoft Excel (Computer file). 3. Libraries—Circulation analysis—Data processing. 4. Collection management (Libraries)—Data processing.
    I. Cooper, Bob, 1963- II. Title.

Z678.88.G74 2007
025.2'10285—dc22   2006101539

ISBN-10: 0-8389-0933-7
ISBN-13: 978-0-8389-0933-1

Printed in the United States of America

11 10 09 08 07   5 4 3 2 1

Contents

Preface

We can think of three reasons you might have decided to read this book. One is that you are a true believer in use studies. The second is that you have heard of use studies and are curious about them. The third is that someone made you. There is a fourth reason: someone in management above you is *not* a believer in use studies, and you are looking for persuasive arguments to do one. Perhaps we can help.

One of the central values of use studies is the concept that each library is unique. Even the common groupings of public, academic, school, and special don't reflect the size of individual libraries and character of the community they serve. Any method of collection analysis that doesn't include how the patrons *use* the collection provides incomplete, and perhaps misleading, data. We do not intend to rehash the arguments for and against conspectus, list-checking, and other nonuse analyses, or to get into the argument about the purpose of a library. Before a library can improve society or learning, or create better schools or better people, it has to achieve this one objective: "exposure of individuals to documents of recorded human experience."[1]

No library has everything. No individual can be exposed to the entire range of human experience. Does your library have the documents your patrons want? Only a use study will tell you.

The best reading, for the largest number, at the least cost.
—The American Library Association motto, coined by Melvil Dewey

Use studies used to be difficult to do. Before circulation systems were automated, researchers had to develop a method of counting use, using checkout cards or the "date due" stamps in the back of the book. Then a valid sample had to be taken, and the results figured. Still, a number of useful and interesting use studies were done, and several are cited in this book. With the advent of the integrated library system (ILS) and, shortly after, the desktop computer, use studies became much easier to do. Ironically, researchers seemed to move away from use studies to investigate database design and computer-human interaction. Still, a number of good studies have been made and continue to be made.

In this book we show how to take decades of ideas in use studies and apply them to your own collection. To do so, we use the popular, powerful, and sometimes maddening Microsoft Excel software program. Although our samples use Excel 2003, the features we use are undoubtedly part of any spreadsheet program you might prefer. The larger ideas we present here are independent of the software we've chosen and will serve you well in any environment.

You can find additional materials, such as sample files, by visiting the ALA Web Extra for the book: http://www.ala.org/editions/extras/Greiner09331/.

NOTE

1. Morris Hamburg, Leonard Ramist, and Michael Bommer, "Library Objectives and Performance Measures and Their Use in Decision Making," *Library Quarterly* 42, no. 1 (January 1972): 111.

Acknowledgments

Any book of this sort owes a debt to many people. First, I want to thank F. W. Lancaster, a longtime advocate of use studies and library evaluation in general. This book would have been far harder to compile without his research and writing. At a personal level, it was Mara Sani who first exposed me to the idea of use studies. She always encouraged her staff to grow and learn, and I am a better librarian for it.

Keith Palmateer, interlibrary loan guru of the Portland Community College Library, tracked down a range of items, once scoring a six-pack off me when he found a particularly obscure work. It is a credit to him that he demurred on the payoff of the bet, asking instead that the money be given to the college's scholarship fund. Jane K. Starnes and Kathleen Johnson were big helps with the arcana of gathering data, and Torie Scott always lent a willing ear to my rambling thoughts on use studies. My most valuable reader was Sue Adams, whose funny and helpful suggestions made this book far easier to understand. My aunt and colleague, Jeannette Carter, gave useful advice about school libraries. May every school in this country have a library and librarian, and soon. Other helpful comments came from Janet Tapper, who saved me from rabbit trouble, and Jane Scott, who provided steady encouragement and thoughtful questions. Support also came from Berniece Owen, Len Anderson, and Donna Meeds. The Tin Shed Tigard Library refugee breakfast bunch have always been stalwarts. Next one's on me.

Darrel Condra of the Tualatin Public Library was way ahead of us on much of this book and gave insight on the politics of use studies. Pat Duke, Jean Peick, and Greg Martin of the Wilsonville Public Library were willing subjects of our experiments. I hope there are not too many scars. Renée Vaillancourt McGrath brought the idea for the book to ALA Editions, and Jenni Fry acted as editor. Copyeditor Carolyn Crabtree made many helpful suggestions and caught more than a few errors. Thanks also to Theresa Yancey, Emily Moroni, Eugenia Chun, Christine Schwab, and the other good people at ALA Editions.

My sweet wife, Mary Grant, encouraged me to take on the project, and lightened the household load whenever she could. She went beyond the call of duty by willingly reading drafts and making suggestions, even though she is blessedly free of library jargon. Of course, this book never would have happened without the help of my writing partner and friend, Bob Cooper. Last, I want to thank those libraries and librarians who have provided the items I have sought through the years, and my parents, who read to me.

—Tony Greiner

First and foremost, I'd like to thank my wonderful wife, Betsy, for inspiring me and giving me words of encouragement when I needed them. To my sons, Ben, whose hilarious personality makes waking up at 6:00 a.m. or earlier to calls of "Wake up, Daddy!" almost enjoyable, and Joe, who was born four days before this book was due—talk about timing. I'd like to thank my parents, Bob Sr. and Ruth, for all of their love and support. Special thanks to my coauthor, Tony Greiner, who is still on friendly terms with me after exchanging over 400 e-mails during the last year while writing this book—yes, I counted them. And, of course, the fine people at Microsoft for creating a very useful program called Excel.

—Bob Cooper

Chapter 1

Books Are for Use

How many books does the library own? How much are the materials used? These are basic questions in librarydom, and while the first is fairly simple to answer, the second gets trickier. One of the tricks in doing use studies is defining a use. Is it a circulation? An in-house use? What if the book is checked out but never read? If a book is used once in its existence, but that use leads to a scientific breakthrough, is it less valuable than a book that was used forty times, but was read only for pleasure? Writers on collection analysis have done a good deal of hand-wringing over these questions, but the short answer is that we don't know how to measure utility, and it's probably impossible to do. Patron satisfaction with a library can be measured with questionnaires and surveys, but valid surveys are difficult to prepare, obtrusive to conduct, and time-consuming. Measuring collection use is comparatively easy to do and has the advantage of having an objective standard.

All libraries would benefit from a use analysis. Even if a patron doesn't pick "the best" source of information for her need, we kid ourselves if we think that reference services and instructional classes reach more than a small fraction of our users. Most people who use a library do so on their own, and the best way we have of determining if they found what they wanted is by seeing if they used something.

> Most libraries that consistently gather data and report progress are the ones whose planning and decisions put them out front, as leaders. They like to know what they are doing, and why.
>
> —Carlton Rochell

For this book, we define a use as a circulation. It is clean and unambiguous, and can be recorded. In some cases the definition of *use* can be expanded to include internal or in-house uses, but it is difficult to get good internal use data. Critics of use studies point out that a circulation doesn't mean the patron found what was wanted or needed, and of course that is true. We are confident, however, that whether a book is read or not read, checked out or used in the library, one thing is clear—use shows patron *interest* in a particular subject or type of literature. And there is evidence that patrons are good at picking out the items they need. In a survey of patrons at the British Science Museum library, 77 percent reported that the material they read answered their information need.[1] The act of taking a book off the shelf signals the library that this item is the type of material the user wants the library to have. The item may or may not fill his need, but the interest is undoubted. A patron who visits a library and walks away empty-handed sends another message, and the former patron who has ceased visiting the library sends the clearest message of all.

Very large libraries with a research mission may be justified in purchasing and keeping rarely used items, but most institutions should look at their collections in terms of how much use patrons made of it. Even those fabled research libraries have clientele who are not themselves involved in research. Undergraduate libraries were created to meet their needs, and for this part of those collections, at least, use should be studied.

A well-done use study can do the following:

1. Gather information for collection development decisions.
2. Assess how the collection is meeting user needs.
3. Determine whether the collection development policy should be amended to meet patron expectations.

4. Reduce subjectivity in materials selection.
5. Identify items for duplication, weeding, or storage.[2]

A lot of ink has been used over the years in discussions of what patrons need as opposed to what they ask for as opposed to what they use. Magrill and Hickey put it this way: "Library users, it is assumed, will communicate their approval or disapproval of the various parts of the collection by their decision to borrow or ignore what the library owns."[3] Or, to put it another way: "Acquisition should be based on *demand* rather than speculation."[4]

There are two main types of collection analysis. One compares a library's holdings with some concept of what the library ought to have, and the other looks at how the library's patrons use its collection. Conspectus and OCLC's "WorldCat Collection Analysis" are examples of collection-based analysis, as are list-checking and buying the *New York Times* bestsellers. There is no doubt in our minds that a collection-based analysis can be useful and productive. However, in the end, what counts is whether or not a collection is used. A 2006 study of the University of Colorado–Boulder found that comparatively few titles accounted for much of the library's use.[5] A use study will reveal if the same is true for your library and will signal the need to buy duplicates of popular titles. More copies of popular books means more satisfied patrons.

A policy of ignoring use and building a collection based on some concept of an ideal collection gives short shrift to current patrons. As we will see later, it is common for items purchased in academic libraries to never receive a use.

> When we have difficulty in determining which books may or may not be used today, the policy of building for the future must seriously be questioned. . . . The future is as much this afternoon as it is the day after tomorrow, six months, a

year or 100 years from now. . . . Budgets, frequently passed on enrollment counts, should be used to fill the needs of the enrollment. If some portion of student fees or tuition is allocated for library materials, this generation of enrolled students may rightfully question a policy which ignores their library needs for the unforeseeable needs of their descendants.[6]

For a very good compilation of collection development and evaluation studies, see Michael Gabriel's *Collection Development and Collection Evaluation: A Sourcebook* and chapter 6 of Lancaster and Sandore's *Technology and Management in Library and Information Services*. School librarians will enjoy *Managing and Analyzing Your Collection: A Practical Guide for Small Libraries and School Media Centers* by Carol Doll and Pamela Barron.

What Should Be Counted?

Use studies look at basic collection measures, including the number and age of volumes, but then they go on to measure circulation, or use, and specifically how much use each part of the collection receives. Various methods of use analysis are presented in chapters 5 to 8.

What Should Not Be Counted?

The idea behind a use study is to find out how your patrons use your library. However, there are always items in a collection that must be retained for political or

Analyzing Library Collection Use with Excel
Contributor(s): Greiner, Tony (Author), Cooper, Bob (Author)
ISBN: 0838909337   EAN: 9780838909331
Publisher: American Library Association
US SRP: $ 40.00 US - (Discount: NET)
Binding: Paperback
Pub Date: January 2007

ET

Author(s)_____

Publisher _____ Date Pub. _____

ISBN _____ Price _____ Edition _____

Vols. _____ Copies _____ Series _____

Requested by _____ Approved by _____
Fill in as much information as possible. Attach publisher ads, catalogs, or book reviews if available.
Return to your library coordinator.
****

LIBRARY USE ONLY

NOTIFY_____MEDIA/BIND: Cloth Paper CD DVD_____

HAVE OLDER ED. _____ REPLACEMENT _____ ADDED COPY _____

VENDOR: B&T ING Alibris _____ PO #____0275320_____

local history reasons, but from which no one expects much use (copies of the local literary magazine, and master's theses, for example). If you have large amounts of this sort of material, remove them from your analysis, so that the comparison of use and holdings size between sections in the library is fair.

Periodicals

Before online magazine and journal databases became commonplace, a number of studies were done of print journal use. We believe that online databases have so changed the nature of periodical use that there is no point in analyzing periodical use with the same steps and procedures as the circulating collection. Indeed, the whole issue of electronic journals and databases is beyond the scope of this book, so it deals solely with analyzing use of books, videos, and other items that physically rest on a library's shelves. For more on electronic journal and database use, see the recommended sources in chapter 10.

Comparing Libraries

The greatest value in use studies comes from comparing use among different parts of a library collection and in tracking changes in use over time. Tracking change over time is especially interesting if the library has made adjustments in its collection procedures to accommodate demand. Libraries that change a collection management policy should analyze use to see if that change did any measurable good. For example, say a use study showed that part of a collection had low total use as well as low use per volume. The collection development specialist then weeded the collection. Certainly use per volume rose after the weed, but did overall use rise after patrons had leaner shelves to choose from? The answer to that question can be provided by a second use study.

Sometimes, however, use numbers are used to compare one library to another. We think that this has marginal utility. There are too many variables in population, mission, and library history to make such comparisons valid. Even if they are of comparable size, comparing Toledo to Tampa is full of difficulty. There may be value, however, in the big picture view of comparing one library's use to the average use of *many* similar institutions. Public librarians who want to view this sort of data can be served by viewing statistical reports by state or referring to the Hennen library survey (http://www.haplr-index.com/HAPLR100.htm) and the Normative Data Project (http://www.libraryndp.info/index.html).

Why Bother Studying Book Use at All? Patrons Want Everything on the Internet

It may seem that way, but a recent study of public library patrons found that about 30 percent came to use the Internet.[7] That means 70 percent came for something other than the Internet: books, videos, a place to read, a storytime. Books are still our business, and they are what the public expects and wants in a library. Public libraries should serve the majority of their patrons by having the books they want on the shelf. School libraries might not purchase on popularity, but they still need to know if their students are using the collection. Academic libraries see heavier online usage than public ones do, but books remain an important and sizable part of their use. In fact, a 2006 study found that even in a computer science collection, books remain an important resource.[8]

There was a time when libraries installed radios in reading rooms and turned them on for important events such as presidential speeches. As radios became common household items, that practice disappeared. We suspect that patron use of the Internet in libraries may be a similar phenomenon. Laptop computers with wireless Internet connections are now common, and it may not be too many years before a home without a fast Internet connection is as unusual as one without a radio. When that day comes, libraries (while still being a supplier of online materials) had better be prepared to meet the demand for what is still our most popular item: books.

Drawbacks and Benefits of Use Studies

As good as they are, use studies aren't perfect. One problem is that it is impossible to weigh the value of a use. A phonebook used five times for a minute can get five recorded uses, whereas a book checked out and read cover to cover gets one.[9] Still, any intelligent look at collection use will recognize those items receive heavy but short-term use. Another criticism of use studies is that the value of a use is unknown. A book may be used only once in its existence, but that use may lead to some great good. This is undoubtedly true and one of the reasons we have large research libraries. But for most libraries, our mission is to serve the people here today, and our budgets and space are too small for us to have the luxury of storing books for a potential user in the possible future.[10]

Martin Faigel said it well:

> Because few of us are blessed with an overabundance of time or staff, and because collection evaluations, rightly or wrongly, have a reputation of being time-

consuming, we often evaluate our collections only in response to external stimuli such as reports needed for an accreditation team. . . . Yet, of course, evaluations of a sort are going on all the time, beginning with the patron checking the catalog for a known item who mutters, "This library never has what I need." . . . Perhaps a major obstacle to our evaluating collections simply for the sake of evaluation is the sense or the certainty that funds will not be available to remedy any weakness that a formal review may document. This is unfortunate, since the rationale underlying any collection evaluation is to discover how well a library is meeting the needs of its users, and it is our professional responsibility as librarians to do so in a systematic way.[11]

Technology has now solved the problem of the cost of collection analysis. By following the procedures in this book, most libraries will be able to analyze their entire collection in no more than a few days, and perhaps a good deal less. Every library has an acquisitions budget. A use study will help show you where to put it. If you want more money for your library, change your collecting to meet demand, watch your circulation rise, and a year or two later go to the funders with the numbers. Funders like success.

NOTES

1. D. J. Urquhart, "The Distribution and Use of Scientific and Technical Information," *The Royal Society Scientific Information Conference, June 21–July 2, 1948, Report and Papers Submitted* (London: The Royal Society, 1948), 408–19, cited in Aridaman K. Jain, "A Statistical Study of Book Use" (PhD thesis, Purdue University, 1967), 144–45.
2. Adapted from Martin Faigel, "Methods and Issues in Collection Evaluation Today," *Library Acquisitions: Practice and Theory* 9 (1985): 22.

3. Rose Mary Magrill and Doralyn J. Hickey, *Acquisitions Management and Collection Development in Libraries* (Chicago: American Library Association, 1984).

4. Charles Osburn, quoted in D. P. Carrigan, "Data-Guided Collection Development: A Promise Unfulfilled," *College and Research Libraries* 57 (1996): 429–37.

5. Jennifer E. Knievel, Heather Wicht, and Lynn S. Connaway, "Use of Circulation Statistics and Interlibrary Loan Data in Collection Management," *College and Research Libraries* (January 2006): 47.

6. William E. McGrath, "Circulation Studies and Collection Development: Problems of Methodology, Theory and Typology for Research," in *Collection Development in Libraries: A Treatise,* ed. Robert D. Stueart, Foundations in Library and Information Science, vol. 10, (Greenwich, CT: JAI Press, 1980).

7. George D'Elia et al., "Impact of the Internet on Public Library Use," *Journal of the American Society for Information Science* 53, no. 10 (2002): 802–20.

8. James Andrew Buczinski, "Debunking the Computer Science Digital Library: Lessons Learned in Collection Development at Seneca College of Applied Arts and Technology," *Acquisitions Librarian* 18, no. 35/36 (2006): 37.

9. Sharon Baker and F. Wilfrid Lancaster, *The Measurement and Evaluation of Library Services,* 2nd ed. (Arlington, VA: Information Resources Press, 1991), 17.

10. We don't agree with it, but for a beautifully written advocacy of libraries having the "best books" rather than responding to user demand, read Carlton Rochell, *Wheeler and Goldhor's Practical Administration of Public Libraries,* rev. ed. (New York: Harper and Row, 1980), 437–40.

11. Faigel, "Methods and Issues," 21–22.

Chapter 2

Excel Basics

In this chapter, you will get a general understanding of how Microsoft Excel works—getting familiar with the terminology and how to navigate around an Excel file. The most common way to open the Excel program is to click on the Start menu at the bottom left of your computer screen, then click on All Programs, and then click on Microsoft Excel. This will open the Excel program and open a blank Excel file. On your computer you may have additional ways to open Excel such as an Excel icon on the Quick Launch toolbar at the bottom of the computer screen. Here are the top terms you need to know in order to work with Excel: *workbooks, worksheets, columns, rows, cells, Formula bar, cell names, Menu bar.*

Each Excel file is called a workbook. When you open a new file in Excel, it will be a workbook comprising three worksheets. Each worksheet has a tab at the bottom that allows you to go from one worksheet to another. Each worksheet is made up of columns and rows, and each column and row is made up of individual cells. A worksheet is made up of many cells. When you click in a cell, the border of the cell becomes bold (see figure 2-1)—becoming the active cell, a cell in which you can add data. As you click from cell to cell, notice how the Name Box changes to show the active cell's location, which is known as its address. When referring to a cell, you should call it by its cell address—for example, A1. An address gives the column first and the row second.

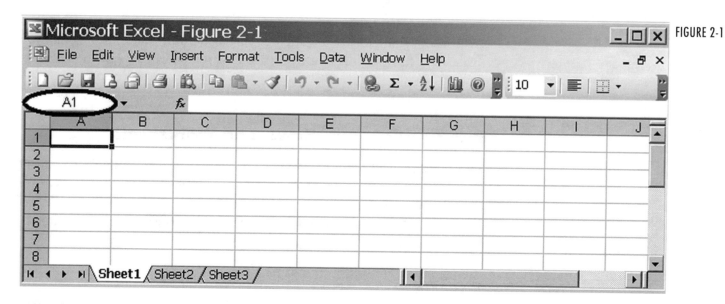

FIGURE 2-1

When working within Excel, there will be times when you have to change your workbook to fit your needs. Most of the changes you will make to your workbook will be done using your Menu bar. If you have worked with other Microsoft products, you may be familiar with some of the capabilities of the Menu bar. There are shortcuts for many of the Menu bar features, such as right-clicking the mouse or using keyboard commands. We will introduce some of these later in the book, but if you are familiar with those, feel free to use them.

The Formula bar is used to perform calculations and insert either information or a function. It is the space to the right of the *fx* (Function) symbol. Functions are ready-made formulas that Excel has created for you to use. You will be using several of these in the upcoming chapters.

The following sections show some common tasks you will need to perform while working in Excel. If you are following along with your own program, you might want to type an X in a few of the cells so you can see how things move around.

Inserting Columns, Rows, and Worksheets

Sometimes you will add information to an existing file. (For example, you might want to create a column that will show the sum of two other columns.) On the Menu bar, click on **Insert** and you see all the items you can insert into a worksheet (see figure 2-2). Functions and charts will be shown in later chapters, but columns, rows, and worksheets are items that you will frequently need to insert.

To Insert a Column

If you want to insert a new column, it will be inserted to the left of whatever column you select. In figure 2-3, we selected column A, and we will create a new column to its left. To create the new column, click on **Insert** and then **Columns** and the new column will appear.

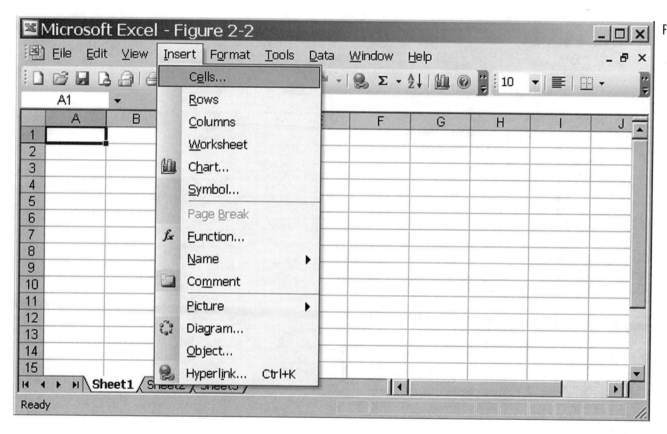

FIGURE 2-2

FIGURE 2-3

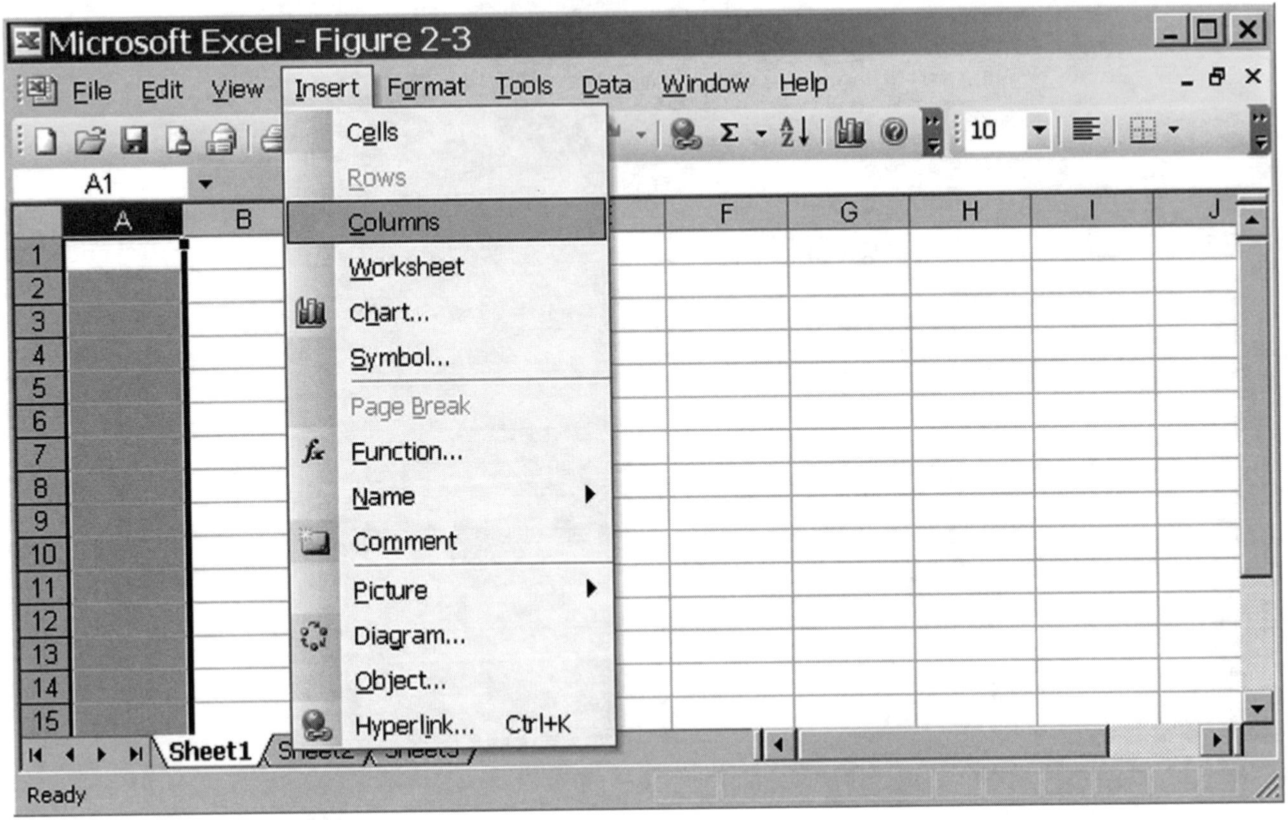
Microsoft Excel - Figure 2-3
File Edit View Insert Format Tools Data Window Help
A1
Cells
Rows
Columns
Worksheet
Chart...
Symbol...
Page Break
Function...
Name
Comment
Picture
Diagram...
Object...
Hyperlink... Ctrl+K
Sheet1
Ready

To Change the Width of a Column

You can change the width of the columns to accommodate the data in them or to "scrunch up" or hide a column that is temporarily in the way. Put your mouse directly on the vertical line separating the letter names of the two columns and click. Notice that the arrow becomes a line with two arrows pointing in opposite directions (+). To make the column wider, simply click, hold, and move to the right. To make it smaller, click, hold, and move to the left. You can actually make a column disappear entirely by moving it so far to the left that it disappears. Do that, and you will notice that the letter name for the column is hidden along with the column. That lets you know there is something under there. To pull hidden columns back out, place the mouse on the line separating the visible columns. Now, instead of a single bar with two arrows, you will see a double bar with two arrows (+). Click on it, hold, and drag to the right, and the hidden column is revealed.

To Insert a Row

To insert a new row, click on the number of the row that you want to place a new row above. Click on **Insert** on the Menu bar and then **Rows** and a new row will appear (see figure 2-4).

FIGURE 2-4

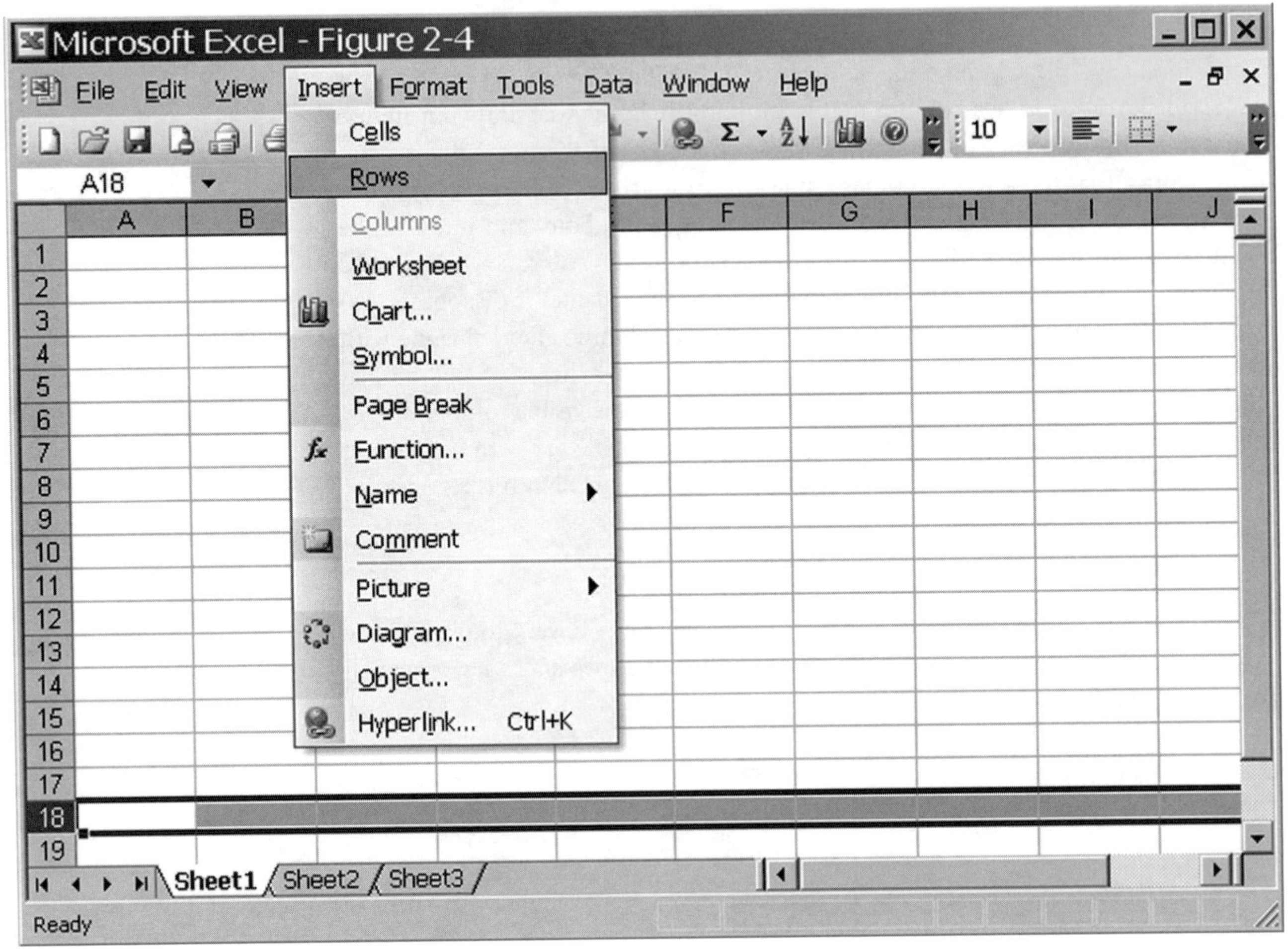

Microsoft Excel - Figure 2-4
File
Edit
View
Insert
Format
Tools
Data
Window
Help
A18
Cells
Rows
Columns
Worksheet
Chart...
Symbol...
Page Break
Function...
Name
Comment
Picture
Diagram...
Object...
Hyperlink... Ctrl+K
Sheet1
Sheet2
Sheet3
Ready

To Insert a New Worksheet

Worksheets have tabs at the bottom of the file. New ones are created in front (to the left) of whichever tab you select. Click on the tab, then click on **Insert** and then **Worksheet** and the new worksheet will appear (see figure 2-5). You can change the name of a worksheet by right-clicking on the tab and selecting **Rename**.

Deleting Columns, Rows, and Worksheets

Sometimes you will want to delete columns, rows, and worksheets from a file. This is a great way to reduce clutter, especially if you are making a presentation to someone. On the Menu bar, click on **Edit** and you will see all the editing features that you can use (see figure 2-6). **Delete** is one of them.

To Delete a Column

Click on the letter name of the column that you want to delete. In the example it is column F. Click on **Edit** and then **Delete** and the column will disappear (see figure 2-7).

To Delete a Row

Click on the number of the row that you want to delete. Click on **Edit** and then **Delete** and the row will disappear (see figure 2-8).

FIGURE 2-5

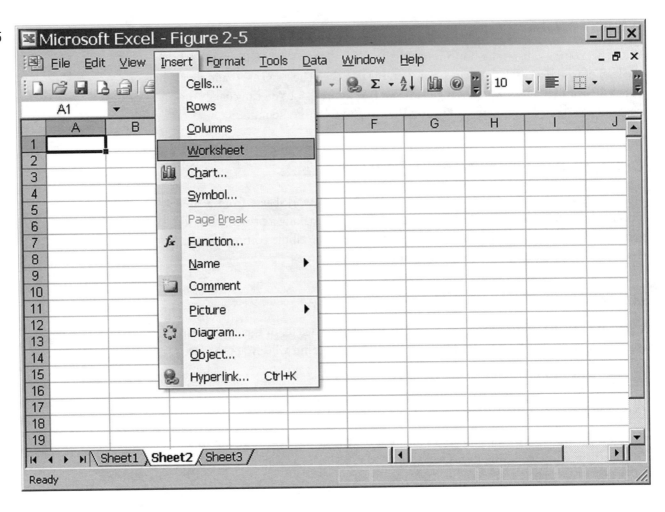

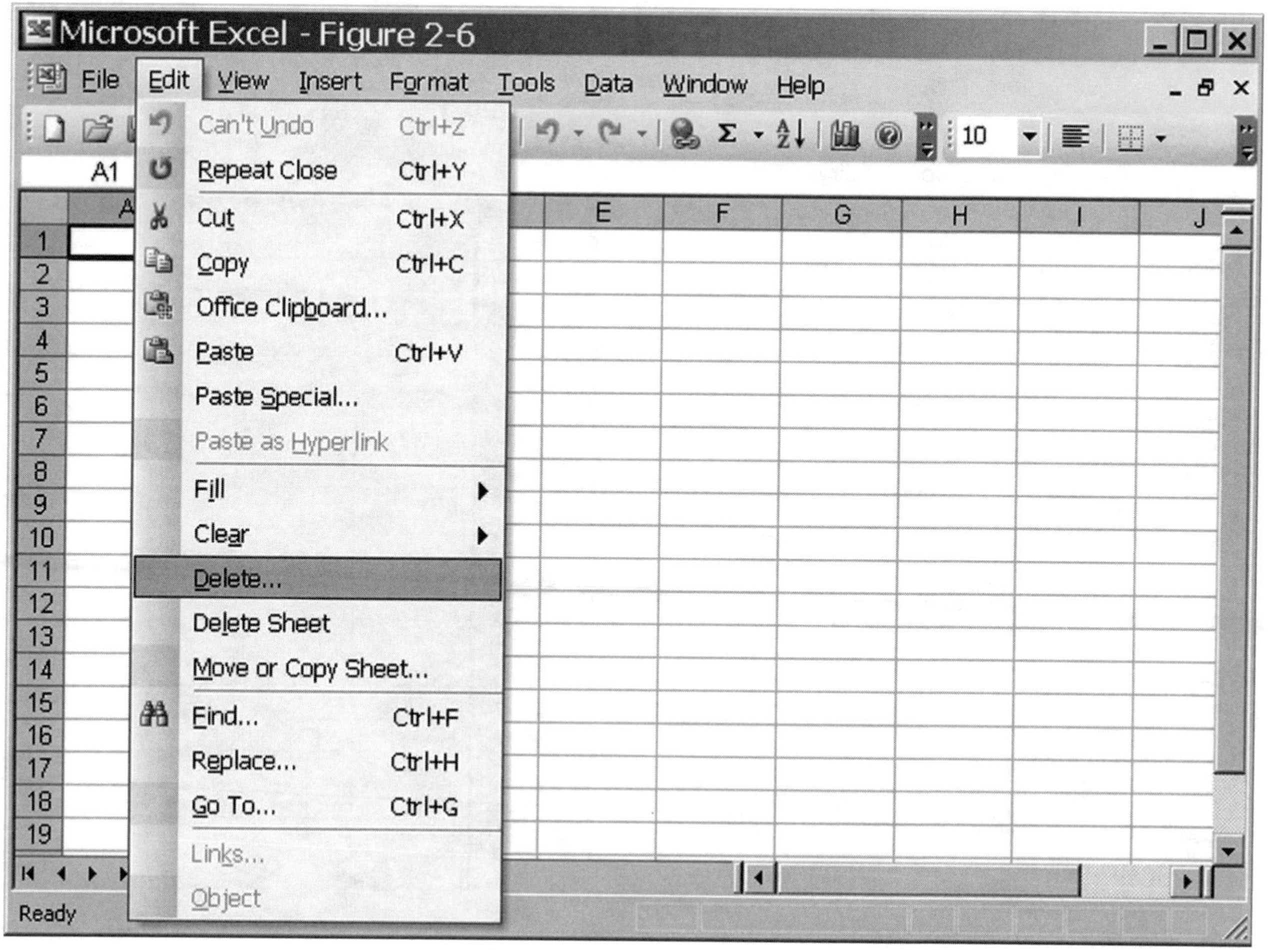
Microsoft Excel - Figure 2-6
File
Edit
View
Insert
Format
Tools
Data
Window
Help
Can't Undo Ctrl+Z
Repeat Close Ctrl+Y
Cut Ctrl+X
Copy Ctrl+C
Office Clipboard...
Paste Ctrl+V
Paste Special...
Paste as Hyperlink
Fill
Clear
Delete...
Delete Sheet
Move or Copy Sheet...
Find... Ctrl+F
Replace... Ctrl+H
Go To... Ctrl+G
Links...
Object
Ready

FIGURE 2-6

FIGURE 2-7

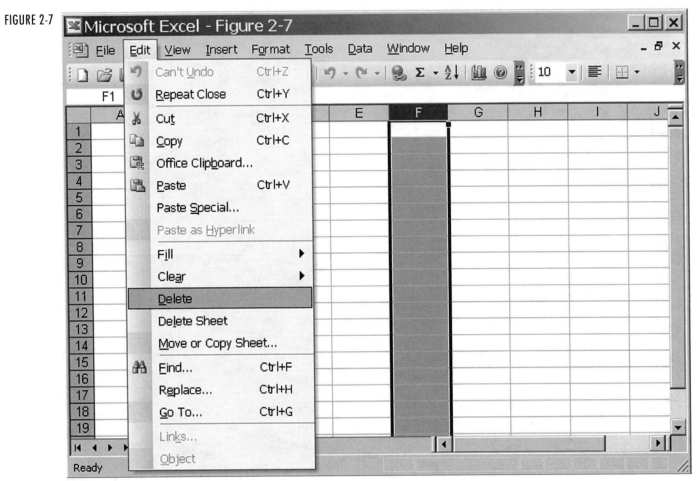

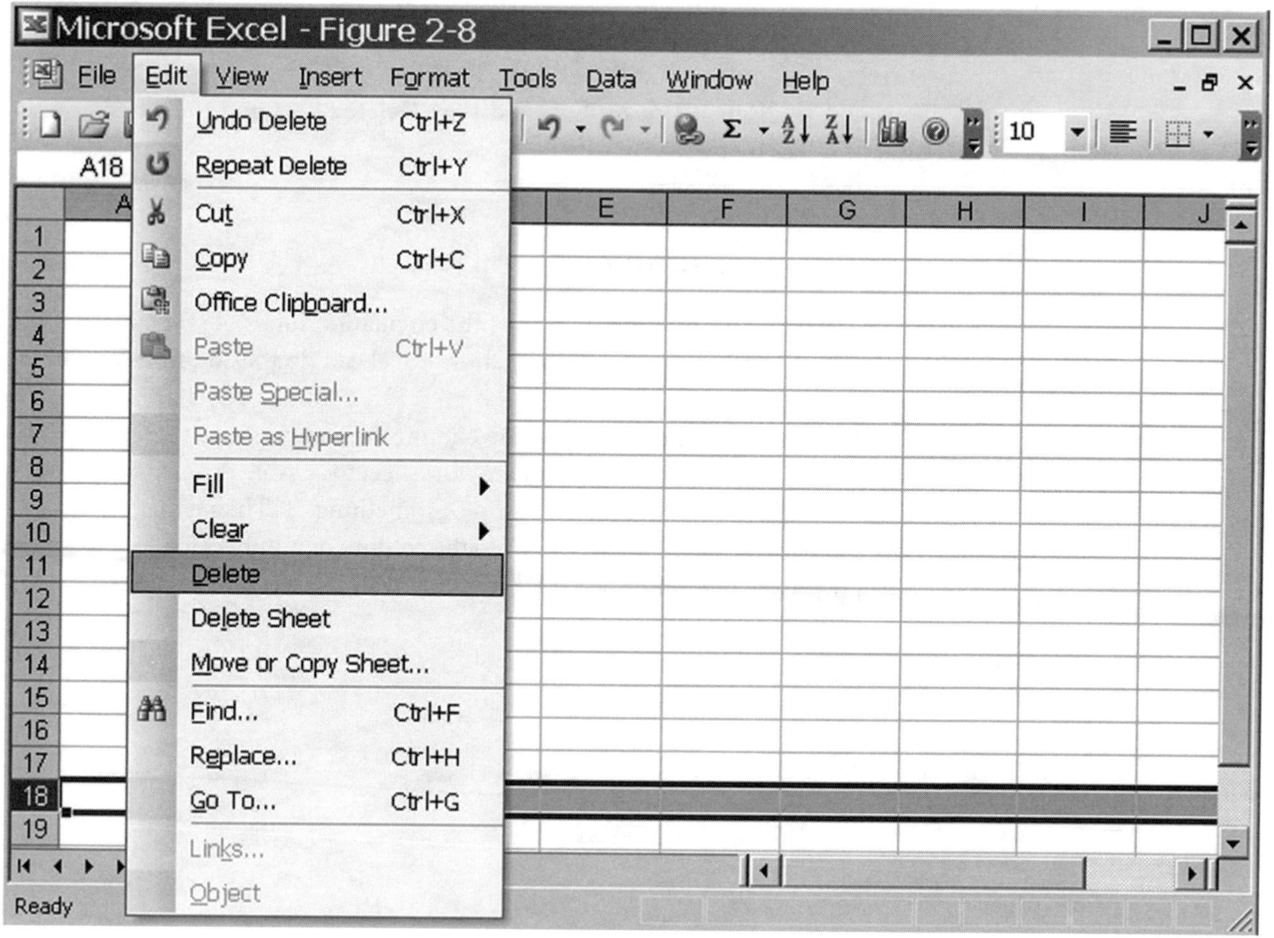

To Delete a Worksheet

Deleting a worksheet is a little different. Click on the tab of the worksheet that you want to delete. Click on **Edit** and then **Delete Sheet** and the worksheet will disappear (see figure 2-9).

Adding a Column of Numbers

If you have a column of numbers, say, the circulation totals of several books, and would like to find out the total circulation, Excel can do the addition for you in a couple of quick steps.

Click in the cell directly below the column of numbers and then click on the sigma (Σ) in the toolbar at the top of the worksheet to activate the AutoSum feature. (Σ is the statistical symbol for "the sum of something.") Then either hit Enter or click Σ a second time, and Excel will add the column of numbers for you (see figure 2-10). If you change a number, it will automatically recalculate the total.

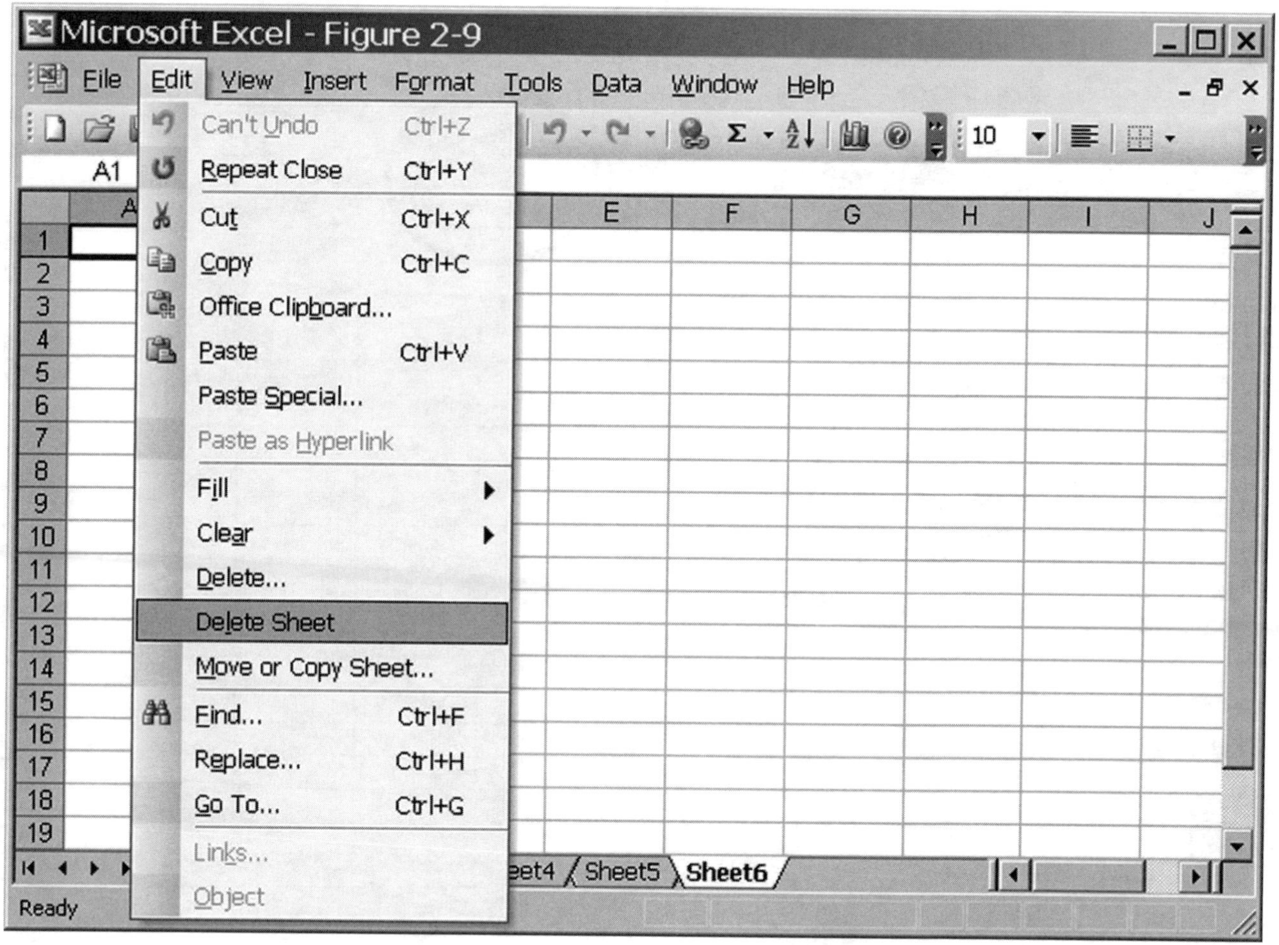
Microsoft Excel - Figure 2-9
File
Edit
View
Insert
Format
Tools
Data
Window
Help
A1
Can't Undo Ctrl+Z
Repeat Close Ctrl+Y
Cut Ctrl+X
Copy Ctrl+C
Office Clipboard...
Paste Ctrl+V
Paste Special...
Paste as Hyperlink
Fill
Clear
Delete...
Delete Sheet
Move or Copy Sheet...
Find... Ctrl+F
Replace... Ctrl+H
Go To... Ctrl+G
Links...
Object
Sheet5
Sheet6
Ready

FIGURE 2-9

FIGURE 2-10

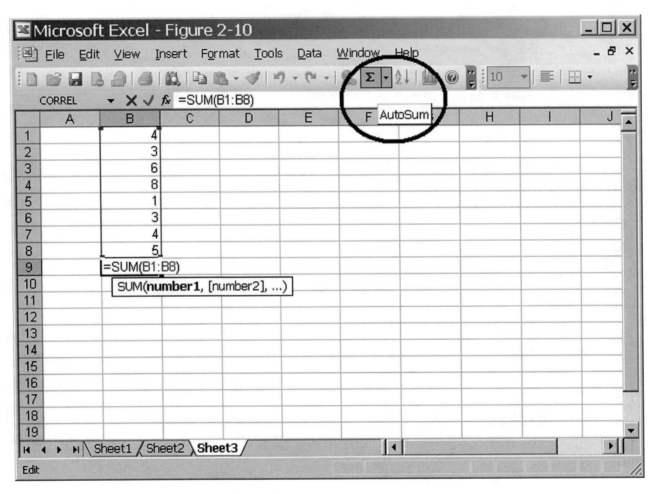

Sorting

Sorting for Excel means putting things in some type of order. In Excel it can be done two ways. One way is to select a column and sort just the items in that column. We don't recommend doing that, because it means that the items that used to be in a row are no longer together. The other way to sort is to organize the entire worksheet by one of the column headings, such as Title, Call Number, or Last Circulation Date. That is what you will do in this book. (You will learn how to add column headings later.)

To sort the entire worksheet, first click on any cell in the column you want to sort by. Then go to the toolbar and click on the button that has the letters A and Z and an arrow pointing down ($\frac{A}{Z}\downarrow$; see figures 2-11 and 2-12). Excel will sort the entire worksheet by the first to last items in the column. You can use the $\frac{Z}{A}\downarrow$ button to sort in the reverse order.

FIGURE 2-11

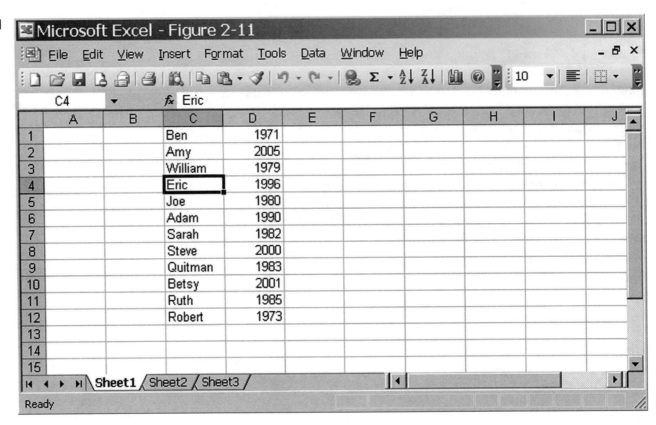

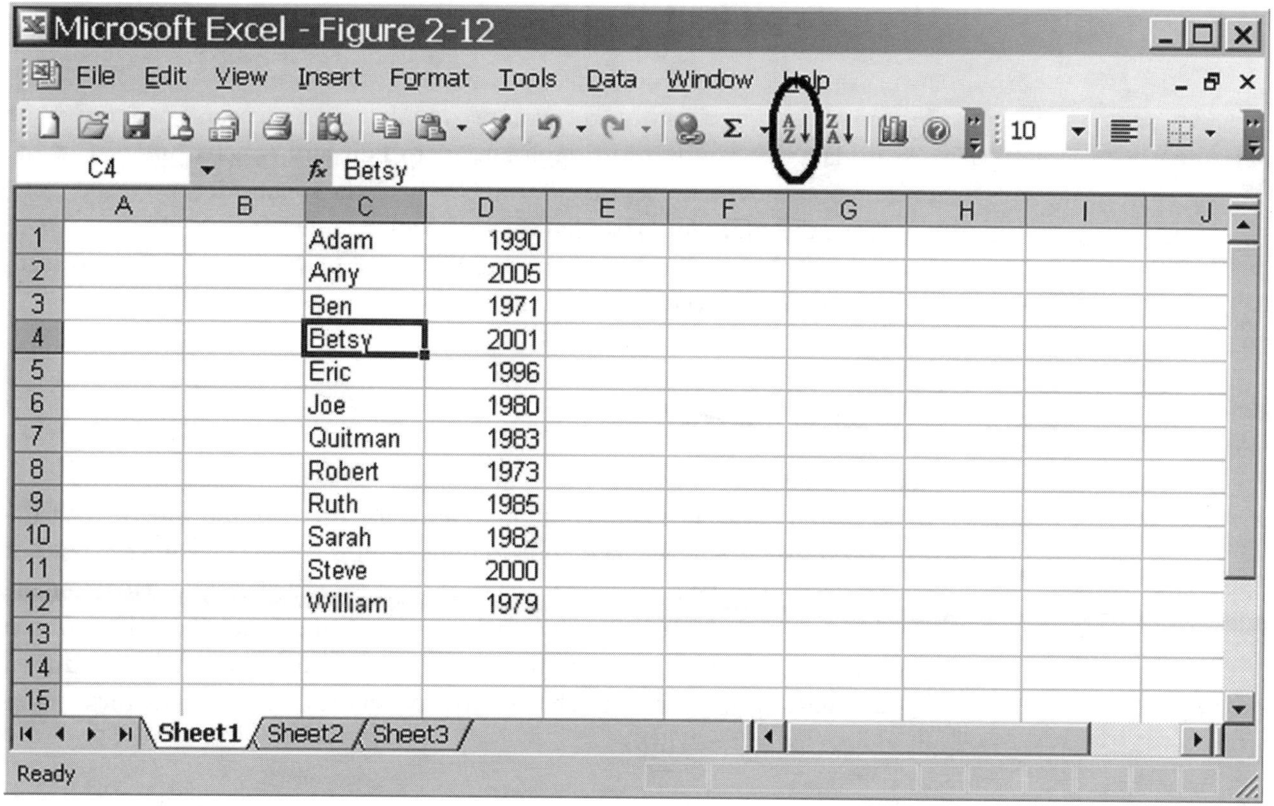
Microsoft Excel - Figure 2-12
File Edit View Insert Format Tools Data Window Help
C4
Betsy
Adam 1990
Amy 2005
Ben 1971
Betsy 2001
Eric 1996
Joe 1980
Quitman 1983
Robert 1973
Ruth 1985
Sarah 1982
Steve 2000
William 1979
Sheet1 Sheet2 Sheet3
Ready

FIGURE 2-12

Using Copy/Cut and Paste

As in other Microsoft products, Copy/Cut and Paste is a very handy tool in Excel. Instead of retyping data or text if you need to move it or repeat it, you can select text or data that you want to duplicate, go to **Edit** and either **Copy** or **Cut** the information—Cut removes the information from the original location, and Copy duplicates the information (see figure 2-13). You then click in the cell or area where you want to place the information, go to **Edit,** click on **Paste,** and the text or data will appear in the new location.

Freezing Rows

Some spreadsheets have hundreds of rows of data, and it can be difficult to remember what each of the columns represents. Freezing the top rows of the worksheet (where you will have your column headings) can help you keep track of your data. To freeze the top rows of the worksheet, first click in the cell that is in the first blank column *and* one row below the data that you would like to have frozen (in the example, cell D2). Go to the Menu bar and click on **Window** and then **Freeze Panes.** You will now be able to scroll down the list and still see the column headings (see figure 2-14).

 TIP With large numbers of rows, Excel sometimes freaks and "freezes" more of the file than you want. An alternative way to keep your column headings visible is to follow the directions under "split pane" in the Help file.

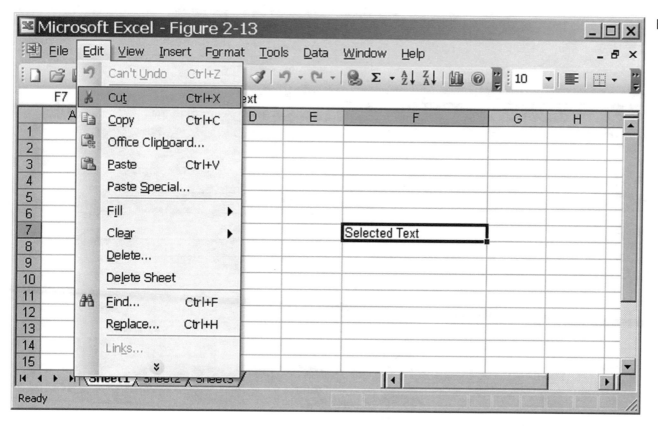

FIGURE 2-13

FIGURE 2-14

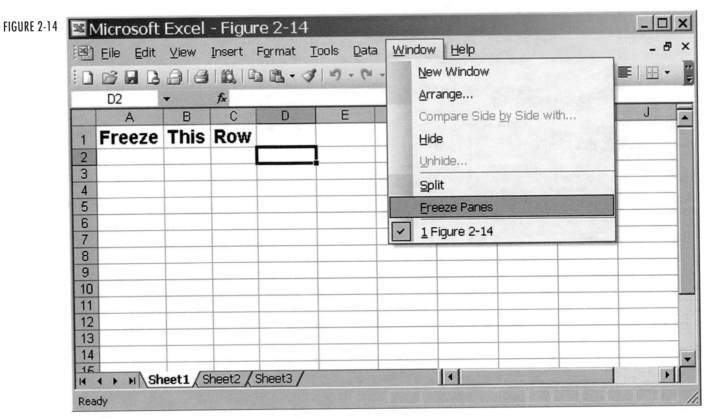

Undoing Text

Under **Edit** on the Menu bar, there is a feature called **Undo Typing.** If you have deleted data on your worksheet and then change your mind and want to keep it, you can click on **Edit** and then **Undo Typing** and the data will return (see figure 2-15). This feature is exceptionally helpful when you have made a mistake. There are times when the Undo Typing feature will not work, but generally it will work until you save the file.

To use this book, you will need to perform additional tasks, which you will learn in the appropriate chapters. We also sometimes present alternative methods of sorting, changing fonts, and the like. Use whatever method works best for you.

FIGURE 2-15

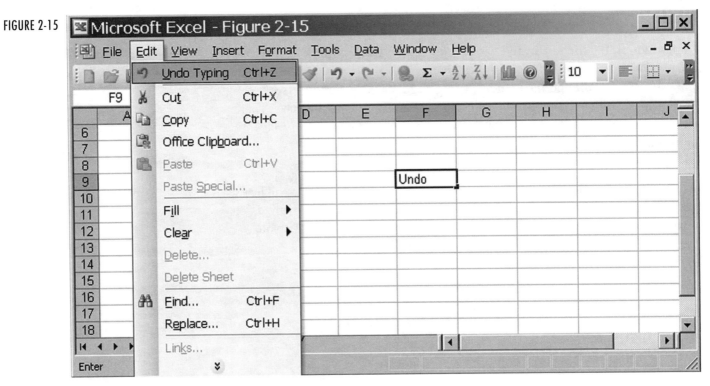

Downloading Data to Excel

The best time to download your data is toward the end of the library's budgetary year. The date is consistent, and if you download at that time, it will be possible to compare that year's budget to use. Depending on your ILS, the size of your collection, and the speed of your desktop computer, the downloading should take no more than a couple of hours, perhaps much less. Fear not, this is like baking bread. Most of your effort is at the beginning and the end of the downloading process. Downloading data a few days before the end of the year is fine, as the goal is to have a "big picture" of use for the entire year. Be sure to download before your system administrator resets the "year to date" circulation numbers to zero!

One of the values of use analysis is that, after you learn how to do it, it isn't particularly time-consuming. This allows for your analyses to be stored and repeated every year or two. The occasion may arise when you want to look retrospectively at something. (Have Stephen King books declined in popularity?) For that reason, we recommend downloading all sorts of data that you may not necessarily analyze right away, or ever. But, as long as you have it tucked away in a master file somewhere, it will be available to you. In chapter 4 we talk about establishing a backup *clean* file and an additional *working* file in which you will do your calculations. It is easy to remove columns of unwanted data from the *working* file when you begin your analysis, but keep them around in the *clean* file, just in case.

Things to Know before Downloading

Call Number Location

An item's call number can be found in one of two places: in the bibliographic record for that item, or on the item record. If your library is part of a cooperative, the call number is probably on the item record (allowing the libraries in the cooperative to have different call numbers for the same title). If your system is stand-alone, it could be either or—worse—both. Talk to your cataloger or system administrator to find out, as it will make a difference in what field you download.

Is Internal Use Recorded? If So, How?

Check whether and how your system records the use of items inside the library. If there is a "total use" field in the item record, does it automatically include internal use? If so, check if there is a "circulation" or "checked out" field separate from "total use." Download the fields you think are appropriate. (For more on the problems and benefits of measuring internal use, see chapter 6.)

Reference, Periodicals, Electronic Books, and Ephemera

You may be able to exclude certain items when you download the collection. Reference items don't normally circulate, so unless you have been scrupulous about recording internal use, there is less to clean out later if you don't download them at all. Use analysis can certainly be run on printed periodicals, but there will be so many items that the files can become very large and clumsy. Periodicals may also skew the numbers on the age of the collection. If you decide to analyze them, do them by themselves as a separate analysis. You should also remove any other items that your system reads as being in the circulating collection, but which, for whatever reason, are not representative of the collection as a whole. (We know of one library that has a MARC record for a Viking broadsword.) We recommend not analyzing electronic books with the print collection because, although they are in the catalog, they are not on the shelves and are never found by browsers. Chapter 5 has a fuller discussion on them. Depending on your ILS, it may prove easier to go ahead and download these items into Excel and cut them out later, but the more extraneous material you can avoid in your initial download the better.

Bibliographic Record or Item Record

You will have the choice of downloading the bibliographic record for the title or each individual item record. Because this is a use analysis, not an analysis of holdings, download the item records. This will lead to a clearer transfer of use data, show use at different locations, and show the status of each item.

Circulation

All systems will have a date of circulation, but for some that is the date checked out and for others it is the date returned. Either checkout or check-in will work for analysis. If your system shows both dates, choose just one to avoid confusion.

Downloading

We suggest downloading as many as possible of the following fields. If your system has some other data that could be interesting, do those as well. Remember that downloading this stuff only means that you will have it available for future reference. You don't use it all in your analysis.

Call number

Title

Author

Location (either a library branch or a subcategory, such as Adult Nonfiction)

Publication or copyright date

Total circulation

Circulation in current year (the one that is drawing to a close as you download)

Circulation in the previous year

Internal use

Total use (circulation and internal)

Last check-in (or checkout) date

Material type (book, video, etc.)

Circulation status (loan period, reference, reserve, etc.)

Catalog date (which will show how long the item has been in the collection)

Status (in, missing, bindery, etc.)

Publisher or imprint

Barcode

There are many ILSs on the market, and although they share basic features, they differ in particulars. Most, if not all, of the systems now on the market can download data into Excel, either directly or through an intermediate step using a text file.

Text files are files with a .txt extension. In these text files, each piece of information is marked off by a "delimiter," which can be a comma, a tab, or any number of other things. Speak with your system administrator about how your system's raw data is organized. Luckily, Excel can convert data from a text file to its own version quite easily. Here is an example.

Imagine you have just downloaded a set of data from your ILS into a text file, which you have given the name *Science.txt*. Now open Excel, and go to **File–Open,** which will open the browse dialog box. Browse to wherever you have placed the *Science.txt* file, select it, and click **OK**. This opens the Text Import Wizard (see figure 3-1). Near the top left, the wizard asks you to choose whether the fields are Fixed width or Delimited. Choose **Delimited,** and click **Next**. Step 2 of the wizard asks you to mark the delimiters. (This tells Excel what mark separates the pieces of information in the text file.) **Tab** is already checked. Check the box for **Comma** as well, and the box that says **Treat consecutive delimiters as one.** (Figure 3-2 shows you what it should look like.) Click **Next,** and on the third step (figure 3-3), just click **Finish.**

FIGURE 3-1

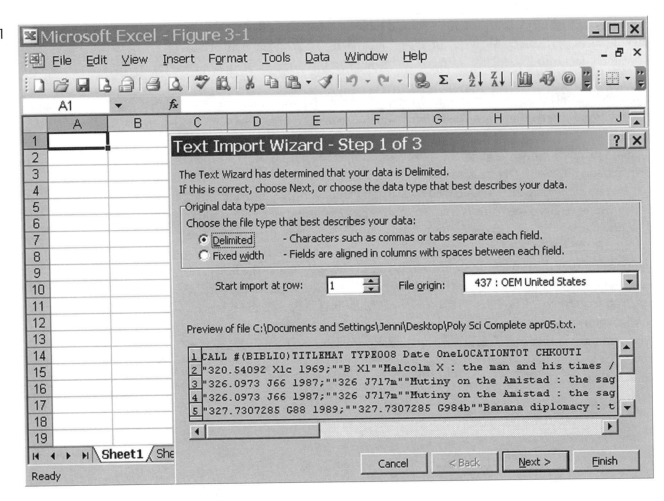

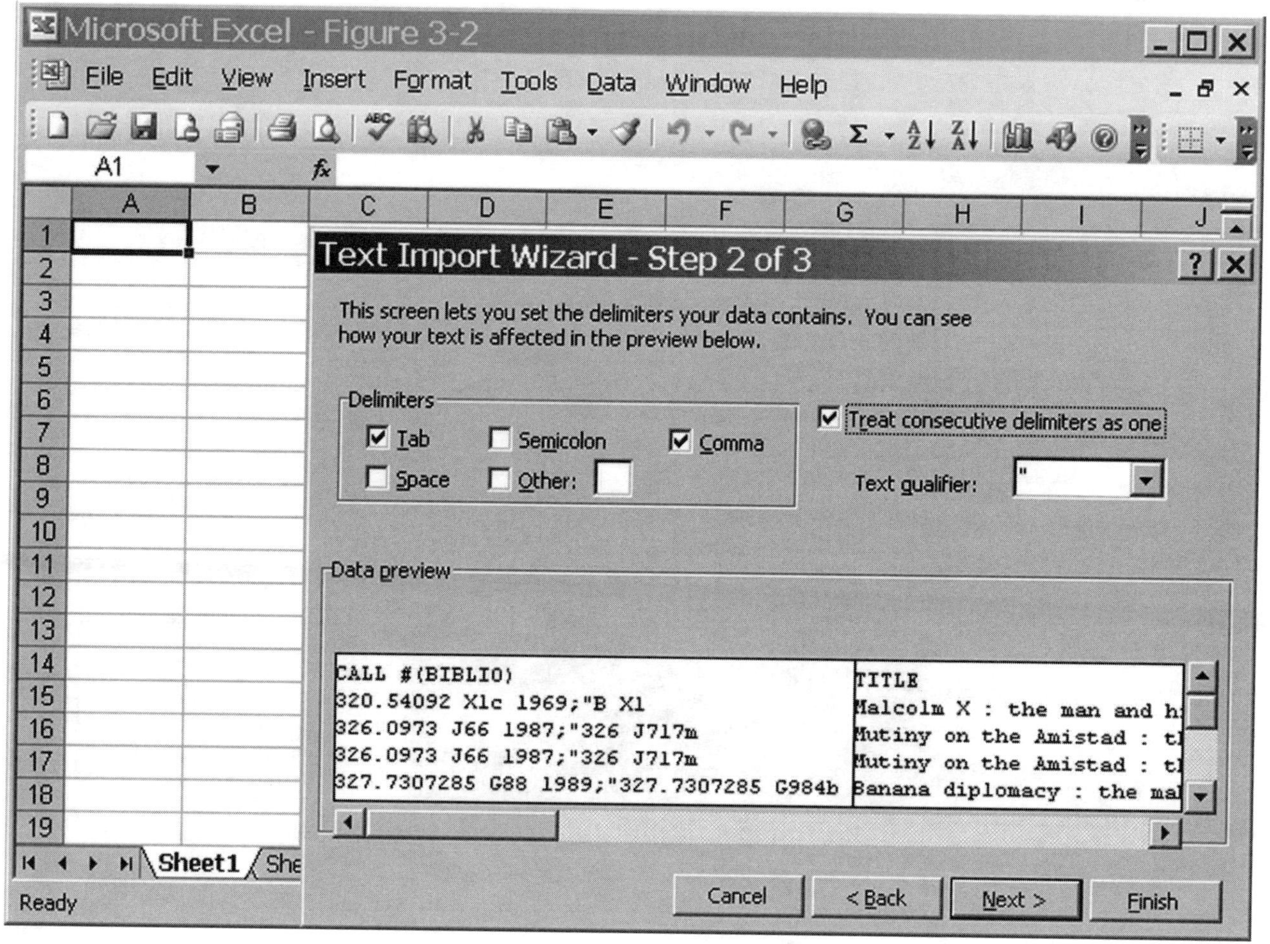

Microsoft Excel - Figure 3-2
File Edit View Insert Format Tools Data Window Help
A1
Text Import Wizard - Step 2 of 3
This screen lets you set the delimiters your data contains. You can see how your text is affected in the preview below.
Delimiters
Tab
Semicolon
Comma
Space
Other:
Treat consecutive delimiters as one
Text qualifier:
Data preview
CALL #(BIBLIO)
320.54092 Xlc 1969;"B Xl
326.0973 J66 1987;"326 J717m
326.0973 J66 1987;"326 J717m
327.7307285 G88 1989;"327.7307285 G984b
TITLE
Malcolm X : the man and h
Mutiny on the Amistad : t
Mutiny on the Amistad : t
Banana diplomacy : the ma
Sheet1
Ready
Cancel
< Back
Next >
Finish

FIGURE 3-2

FIGURE 3-3

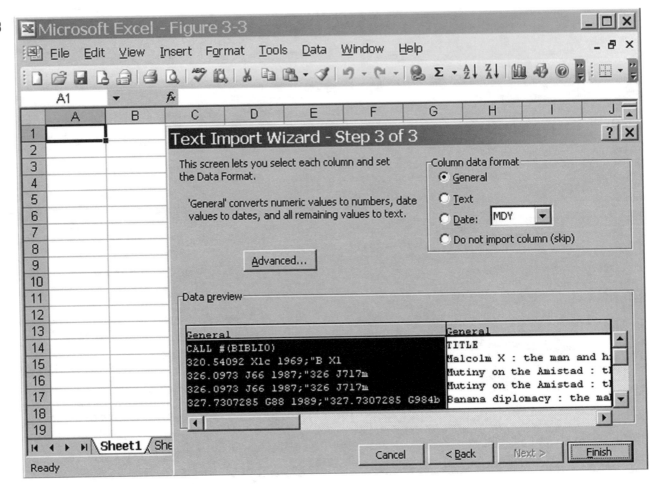

The Excel file will now open, reading the data from your text file. Notice that the file extension is .txt, not .xls, the normal Excel extension. More on that in a minute. If you have a mess, close and discard the file and repeat the process, trying some other delimiters. If things worked, the different fields you downloaded (Title, Call number, Author, etc.) should now appear as headings for each column. If you see cells with # signs, it means there is more information in the cell than fits in the available space. Expand the width of the cell (see chapter 2) until the data is readable. Columns with long strings of numbers, such as the Barcode column, will often be expressed in scientific notation. To change them to regular numbers, highlight the Barcode column by right-clicking on the letter name for that column and select **Format Cells** (see figure 3-4). Under the Category heading, click on **Number.** Notice that a new box, labeled Decimal places, appears. Toggle the number down to zero, and click **OK.** The numbers will now be in regular format. (The tabs in the Format Cells feature can be used to change fonts and other things as well.)

There are always some foul-ups when data is transferred. If the data was basically transferred correctly, these errors will be in the form of "extra" cells that don't fit in a column. It will be necessary to "clean up" these errors before an analysis can be done, as will be explained in chapter 4.

Different versions of Excel have different limitations on the amount of data that you can import. Excel 2000 and Excel 2003 have limits of 256 columns and about 64,000 rows. Excel 2007 has a limit of 16,000 columns and 1,000,000 rows. If you are studying a collection larger than that, break it up into smaller sections by call number or format before downloading.

FIGURE 3-4

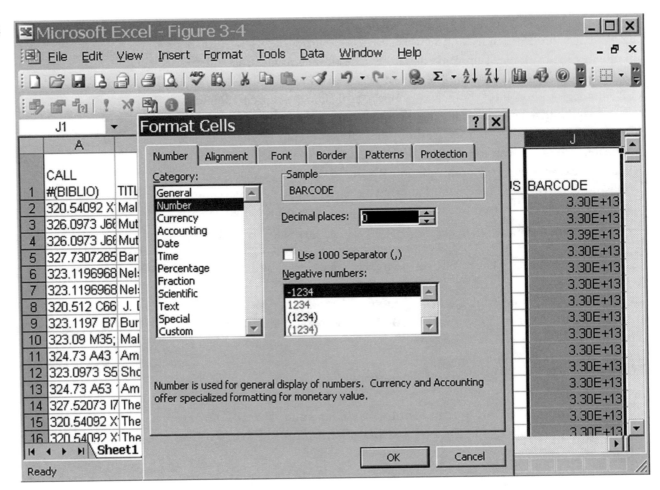

Remember that this is a text file (.txt) rather than a true Excel file. You will need to convert this data into a true Excel file. To do so, you first close the file by clicking on the smaller X in the upper right-hand corner (see figure 3-5). A dialog box will appear, asking if you want to save your changes. Click **Yes.** Another dialog box will appear, asking if you want to keep the workbook in that format. Click **No.** Excel immediately gives you the opportunity to save the file in the Excel format by showing a **Save As** box that has the name of the file changed to one with a .xls ending (see figure 3-6). Now you can use the drop-down menu at the top of the dialog box to place the file in a folder, and you can change the file's name. We recommend keeping this file as raw data—not cleaned up at all. Change the name to *Science raw.xls* (or whatever is appropriate), and click **Save.** The file closes, but Excel remains open. Now go to **File–Open** to locate the file again by its new name, and open it up. It is now in the Excel format.

One last thing to do: now that the file is open again, go to **File–Save As** and give it a new name one more time, calling it *Science clean.xls.* This will be the version that you clean up, saving the raw version in case something goes wrong. More on that in chapter 4.

FIGURE 3-5

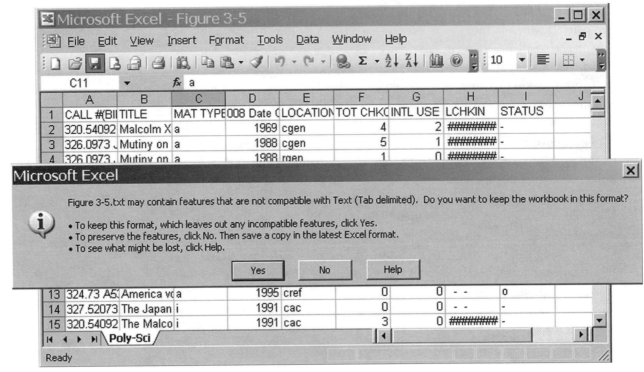

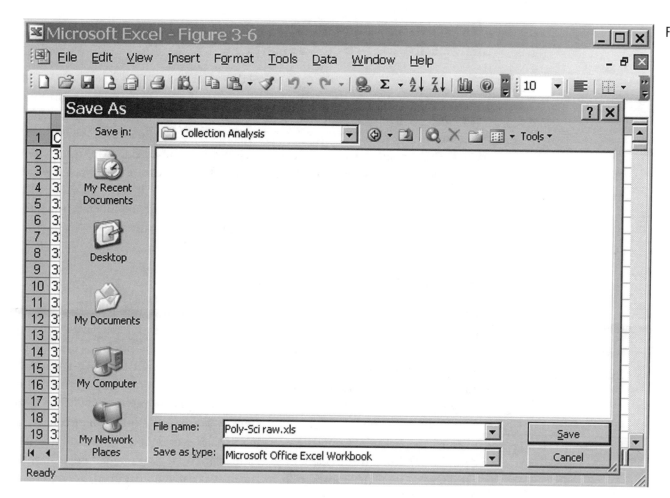

FIGURE 3-6

Downloading from Specific Integrated Library Systems

There are many ILSs, and the methods of downloading data are sure to change, so we are not including directions on downloading in this book. If you are so fortunate as to have a database administrator with whom you can work, she or he can show you how to download. Unfortunately, most manuals remain incomprehensible. If you have clear and complete directions on how to download data from your system into Excel, please visit the ALA Web Extras website for this book, http://www.ala .org/editions/extras/Greiner09331/. Visit the site to see if directions for your ILS are available and to download some sample files to play with as you go through the rest of this book. Our e-mail is excelbook@gmail.com.

Vendor-Supplied Analysis

Because this is the chapter on downloading, this is the time to talk about the possibility of purchasing a vendor-supplied use study. All systems have some sort of method of creating statistical reports of circulation data. The ones we have seen are aggregate—they can show how many items were checked out on a given day, and how many over the year, but not what those items were. This information is certainly useful for library management, but it doesn't address details of collection use. However, some ILS vendors (for an extra fee) are starting to offer collection use analysis packages. Contact your system's sales representative and see what use data the vendor can provide and how much it costs. You might find that your vendor can supply the information you need at a cost you can afford, or you might decide to stick with the methods in this book.

The Follett Company, which targets school libraries, has a product called Titlewise. Titlewise is free for customers of Follett Library Resources, their book-selling division. Titlewise can generate charts and graphs showing the number of books per student and the number and average age of the items for categories such as easy readers and audiovisual, as well as for each Dewey 10. In addition, the product compares the library's holdings by category with recommended size and age lists created by both Follett and H. W. Wilson. Good stuff at no extra charge, but as good as it is, Titlewise does not analyze use. We want to encourage other ILS vendors to follow Follett's lead, but even Follett customers will benefit from giving their collections a use analysis.

Chapter 4

Cleaning Up the Data

In most cases when you export data from a library system into Excel, there will need to be some data cleanup. Once you have your data exported into Excel, the first thing you want to do is save your original import and keep the original worksheet untouched. Give it a good identifying name, such as *Science Raw Data 2008.xls.* Then go to **File–Save As** and make a second copy with the name *Science Clean 2008.xls.* This will be the copy that will be cleaned of errors and miscellaneous entries. After you have cleaned up this file, create a third copy, called *Science 2008 Working.xls.* The actual analyses will be done from the working file. One reason for making all these copies is that you do not want to have to repeat the export if you make a mistake along the way. If you make a mistake in the working file and can't correct it, you can always go back to the clean file to begin again.

There is another reason to have the clean file as a backup. Excel is one of those software programs that sometimes decides it knows what to do better than you do. As a result, it will occasionally insert formulas where you don't want them, make random changes in formatting, and perform other maddening acts. Sometimes these can be cleaned up by the user, but other times they create such a mess that it is easier to shut it down and start all over again. Having an untouched clean file is worth the little bit of extra work.

Removing Extra Cells

Go to the clean copy you just created. More than likely there are some "extra" cells that are not lined up with your column headings. Everything must be in the correct column before you can do an analysis, so this is how to get everything lined up. Go to **Data–Sort.** Make sure you have selected **Header row** at the bottom of the dialog box. (These are the column headings such as Title.) If somewhere in the file there are extra cells spilling over to the right of your last heading, the Sort by drop-down menu will have the letter names of these "extra" columns (see figure 4-1). Do a sort by the first column *after* the last column with a heading. (In other words, if your last column with a heading is Barcode, and the next column to the right is column K, then sort by column K.) This will bring the items with "extra" cells of information up to the top. Now don't follow your impulse to just delete those extra cells. The problem is probably located to the left of the extra cells, where there is an unnecessary blank cell, odd symbol, or repeated term filling a cell. The thing to do is eliminate these unwanted cells, so everything else gets in the correct column. In figure 4-2, there are two rows with the author's name repeated in a neighboring cell. Select, then right-click on those repeated cells, then choose **Delete** and **Shift cells left.** This will erase the repetition and bring the dates into alignment under the column titled Year.

It is best to use the right-click to delete rather than using the Delete key because the right-click allows you the option of shifting the cells. If for some reason deleting is not a good option, you can right-click and select **Clear Contents.** This removes whatever is in the cell, but doesn't shift anything around. If you make a mistake, a handy thing to remember is the **Edit–Undo** command (see chapter 2). Go ahead and delete the "bad" cells from your clean file, or download the practice file for

FIGURE 4-1

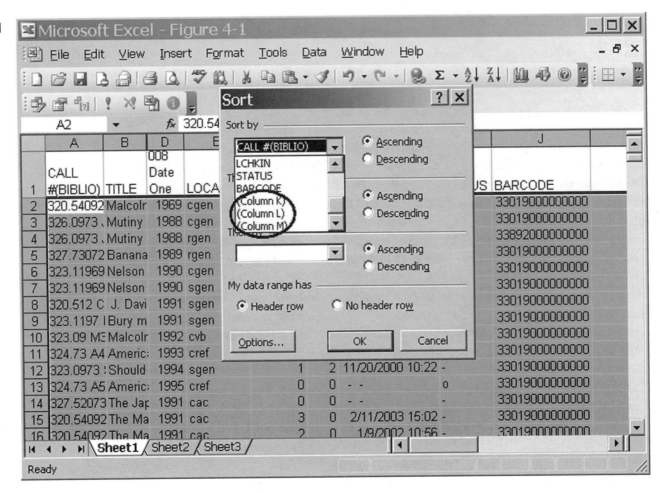

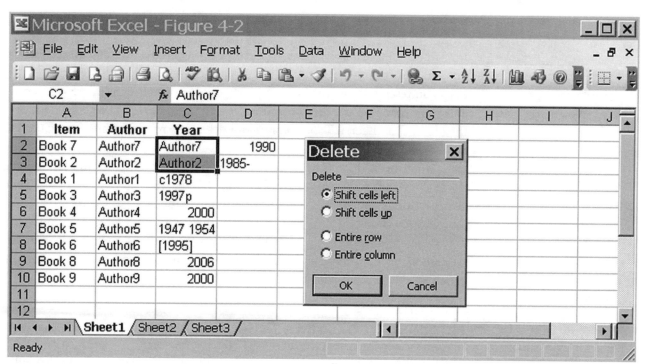

FIGURE 4-2

this chapter (4) from http://www.ala.org/editions/extras/Greiner09331/. You might have to repeat the sorting and deleting process a couple of times before you have removed all the extra cells. You will know you have cleaned up the extra cells when the Sort by choices no longer include a column with a letter name.

Removing Unwanted Item Records (Rows)

In a large file, there may be items that really are not part of the circulating collection, but which somehow got into the file. Magnifying glasses, earphones, and private books on reserve sometimes show up. After you have removed the repeated cells, and everything is in the correct column, it is time to get rid of this ephemera. Sort the file by the Material Type column and delete the rows of items that you don't want to include in the analysis. If you have several items grouped together that you want to delete, click on the first row number in that group, hold, and scroll down the list of row numbers until you have highlighted all the offensive items. Then switch to a right-click and delete them all, moving the other rows up.

Next you want to clean up the dates in the Publication Date column so they are considered numbers and not text. As long as there is anything in the date column that is not a number, Excel will be unable to add or do other mathematical functions. Dates are usually the trickiest part of cleanup.

Handling Publication Dates for Items in a Series

There is one step you have to do before cleaning up the dates automatically. Some items that are issued serially (such as the Best Short Stories series) will have catalog records that show only the date of the first item in the series, followed by a hyphen. (For example, the book *Best Short Stories of 2006* will have a MARC record that shows the date as "1933-" where the dash indicates, in this case, that the item is part of a series that began in 1933.) If you let the 1933 date stand, then that date will be used in calculations for the age of the collection. You don't want to have that grossly incorrect date in the file. You have two choices. One is to manually correct the dates by typing the correct date into the cell. This isn't hard if your file is not particularly long.

If the file is so large that this makes you want to pull your hair out, another option is to just clear the contents of those cells, so that no date is read at all. Although less than ideal, the file you are working in is probably large enough that when you eventually do analyses such as average age, your sample will still be statistically valid. The easiest way to find these items from series is to sort the file by call number. Then look in the Year column for dates followed by a hyphen. They will tend to be gathered into groups because all the items in the series (Best Short Stories) will have the same call number. This sounds more tedious than it is. If you have a whopping big file, you can delegate a lot of these cleanup details.

Cleaning Up Extraneous Symbols in the Year Column

Now that you have made your decision on the items from a series, it is time to remove the various letters and symbols that populate the Year column. Highlight the Year column (just the Year column) by clicking on the letter name of the column, then click **Edit** on the Menu bar and then **Replace.** In the **Find what** field, type in one of the unnecessary symbols that are found in the Year column: c, <, p, and anything else that isn't a number. Leave the **Replace with** field empty. Click **Replace All** and the unwanted symbol will disappear from the entire column (see figure 4-3). Repeat as often as necessary to clean out the extraneous stuff.

FIGURE 4-3

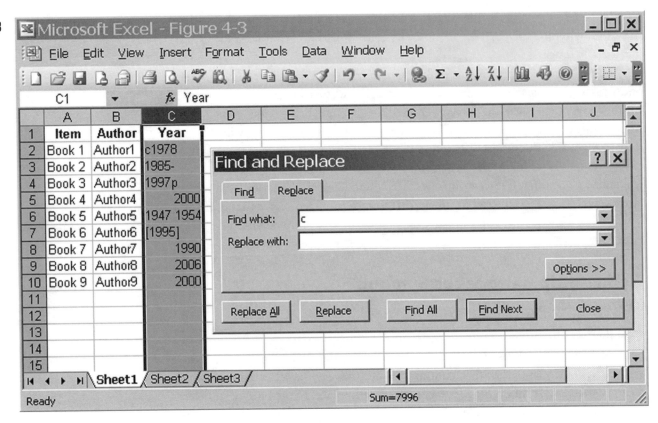

Catalogers sometimes put a question mark after a date to indicate that they are making an intelligent guess. This approximate date is good enough for our purposes and can be used. However, do not put in the question mark (?) as a Replace item. The question mark is a wild card and will replace all data in all the selected cells. To remove question marks in the Year column, add a tilde (~) before the question mark, so the Replace field will show "~?" but will actually remove only the question mark.

For the more adventurous analyzer, you can have a Visual Basic script do this part of the cleanup for you. (Skip this next section if you are happy with cleaning those extra symbols by hand.) Here is the script:

```
Function ExtractNumber(rCell As Range)
Dim iCount As Integer, i As Integer
Dim sText As String
Dim lNum As String
sText = rCell

    For iCount = Len(sText) To 1 Step -1
        If IsNumeric(Mid(sText, iCount, 1)) Then
            i = i + 1
            lNum = Mid(sText, iCount, 1) & lNum
        End If

        If i = 1 Then lNum = CInt(Mid(lNum, 1, 1))
    Next iCount

ExtractNumber = CLng(lNum)
End Function
```

You can also get the script online at http://www.ala.org/editions/extras/ Greiner09331/ if you want to copy and paste the script instead of typing the whole thing in.

Step 1. After you have cleaned up the data to the point of cleaning up the dates, insert a column next to the Year column.

Step 2. Hit Alt+F11. Then click on **Insert** and then **Module** (see figure 4-4).

Step 3. Copy and paste the script into the pop-up box and hit Alt+Q (see figure 4-5).

Step 4. We want the results adjacent to the original data, so in the example we selected cell D2. Next, click on *fx,* then choose **User Defined** from the drop-down menu (see figure 4-6).

Step 5. Select the function **ExtractNumber** and click **OK.** Enter the first cell location in the pop-up box—i.e., C2—and click **OK**. The results will appear in column D (see figure 4-7).

Step 6. Click and drag the little box in the bottom right corner of the cell and it will populate the numbers all the way down (see figure 4-8).

This script cleans out all the nonnumerical symbols, but you will still have to deal with cells that have two dates in them.

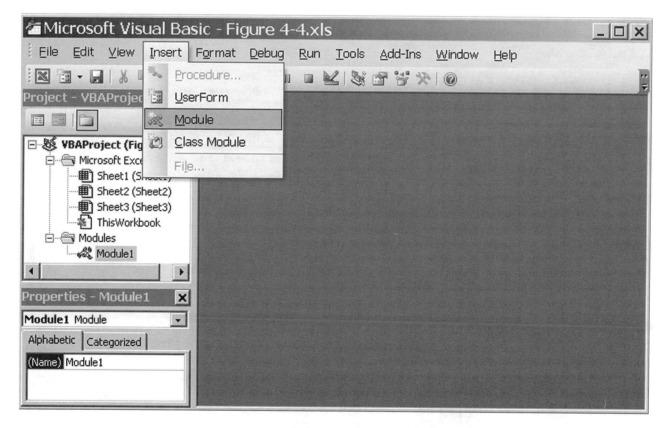
FIGURE 4-4

FIGURE 4-5

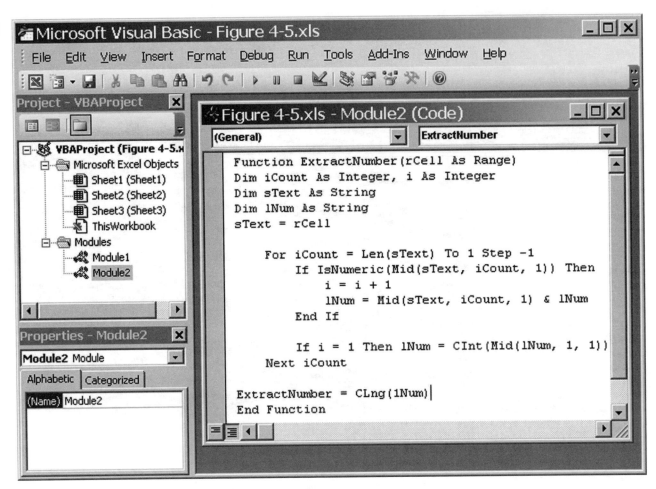

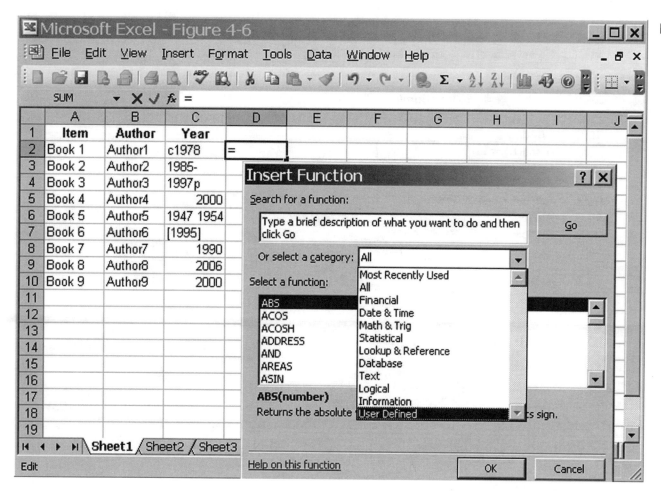

FIGURE 4-6

FIGURE 4-7

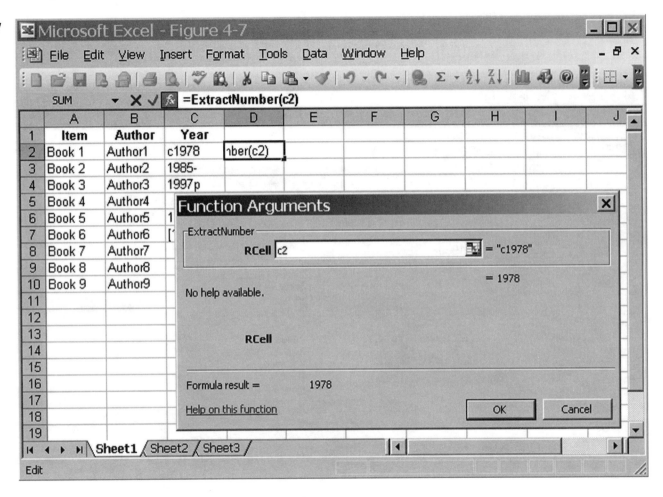

FIGURE 4-8

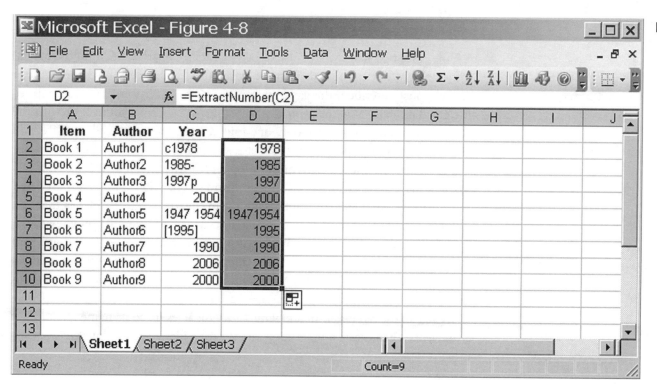

	A	B	C	D	E	F	G	H	I	J
1	**Item**	**Author**	**Year**							
2	Book 1	Author1	c1978	1978						
3	Book 2	Author2	1985-	1985						
4	Book 3	Author3	1997p	1997						
5	Book 4	Author4	2000	2000						
6	Book 5	Author5	1947 1954	19471954						
7	Book 6	Author6	[1995]	1995						
8	Book 7	Author7	1990	1990						
9	Book 8	Author8	2006	2006						
10	Book 9	Author9	2000	2000						

D2 = ExtractNumber(C2)

Cleaning Cells with Two Dates

In some cases two dates will be listed, perhaps for a paperback edition or reprint. Unfortunately, one of those dates must be removed by hand. Note that if you run the script just described, the gap between two dates disappears, and you will see an eight-digit date. Whether you clean up the Year column yourself or with the script, it is important to leave only one four-digit date in each cell, or Excel will think the book was published in 18562002. We recommend using the most recent date. If you have a 2005 reprint of *The Origin of Species,* call it a 2005 book. It will look new, have an up-to-date introduction, and so on. Your library has purchased a new printing, showing continuing interest in this title, and the idea is that you are buying books that meet your patrons' interest. In addition, if you go with the date of original publication, then you will need to have 2000 BC for Homer and 1598 for Shakespeare. Removing the extra date is a good job for student workers or volunteers. Sort the file by the Year column, so the rows with two dates in them will be grouped together and can be easily cleaned up.

When all the data is clean and your *Clean* file lives up to its name, do another **Save As,** and then create a third copy, the *Working* file to use for your analyses.

Chapter 5

Determining the Size and Age of Your Collection

his chapter deals with basic collection analysis information, and it will also help you set up your *Summary* file, in which you compare your findings for the various parts of your collection. Refer to your ILS manager (or manual, heaven help you) and chapter 3 to learn how to download information from your system. Begin by deciding what part of your collection you want to analyze (typically a call number range, or, for fiction, perhaps a genre such as mysteries). If you are doing an analysis that covers several different call number ranges (for example, "business and investing" with call numbers from economics, finance, and management), you may need to download several call number ranges and then cut and paste them together into a new Excel file. Clean up the data following the directions in chapter 4. Now you are ready to begin to analyze your collection. Be sure to do a **Save As** command and save a third copy of the file as your *Working* file, for example, *Business and Investing, working 2008.*

Whenever you can, count.

—Sir Francis Galton

Deciding What to Analyze

Decision 1: Missing and Lost Items

Libraries tend to let items in "missing" and "lost" status linger for years. If that is the case for your institution, we recommend removing the records for items in "missing" or "lost" status from your *Working* file. The idea is to analyze the collection your patrons can actually use. If you work in an institution that cleans its data every year, then go ahead and count these items, as they were available for some of the year you are analyzing.

Decision 2: Reference Items

Depending on your ILS, sometimes it is easier to download reference and circulating items together. The advantage of doing this is that you can see the age, volumes, and so on of your collection as a whole. However, it is best to remove the noncirculating items from the file before you begin your circulation analysis. Cut and paste the reference item records into another file called *Reference*, and analyze their use and age separately, or analyze your reference collection as a whole, or not at all.

Decision 3: On Order and In Processing Items

Remove "on order" and "in processing" status items from your *Working* file. These items will lower your average use figures, and your patrons have not yet had access to them. You can certainly set them aside in another file and count them as part of items purchased, but not as part of the used collection. You will need to remember to move them back and forth as needed. We suggest putting a note to yourself on what you did directly in the Excel file, somewhere below the data. Then, next year, you don't have to remember.

Decision 4: Mending, Bindery, and Other Items

Assuming they are processed and returned to the shelves fairly quickly, items in "mending" or "bindery" status should be counted as part of the active collection, as they were probably present for most of the year being analyzed. If you have a tech services department that measures time in geologic ages, consider and count "mending" and "bindery" items as unavailable (more on that later) and remove them. Check also for items with an unusual status, such as "on librarian's desk," and remove or keep them as you see fit. Remember to do these cuts from your *Working* file. Someone may ask you for information about missing materials later, and if you have them in your *Clean* file, they will be easy to find.

Decision 5: Electronic Books

For several reasons, electronic books are a problem area in collection analysis. First, electronic books are often purchased in packages, so for economic reasons, use of the package as a whole needs to be considered. Second, depending on the vendor, there is a range of criteria that are called a "use," including clicking on the title, downloading pages, or "checking the book out" to a personal computer. Some vendors count every separately viewed file as a use. A reader who looks at an e-book with text, a graph, and a photograph will record three uses, whereas someone using the print version will record only one. Last, although electronic books are in your catalog, they are not on the shelves and are never found by browsers. At this writing, we think it best to look at electronic books separately and not include them in your analysis of your print collection. If you decide to include electronic books in your analysis of print materials, make sure that your definition of "use" for the print collection is the same as it is for an electronic book. See chapter 10 for more on electronic books.[1]

Creating a Summary File

As you proceed with your collection analysis, you will need a place to record your data. Create a new and separate Excel file, giving it a name like *Collection Analysis Summary 2007*. Keep your *Summary* and your *Working* file open as you go along, as you will be transferring information from one to the other. The *Summary* file will start with four columns. The first column identifies what part of the collection you are talking about, the second records the number of items in that section, the third lists average publication date, and the fourth shows median publication date, which you will learn about in a minute.

When transferring numbers to your *Summary* file, you can either cut and paste from the *Working* file, or just retype the numbers. The cut and paste version creates a link between the two files, so that if the data in the *Working* file changes, it also changes in the *Summary* file. This is tempting but can cause problems. Think back to those times when Excel starts doing things on its own. If you used the cut and paste method, your *Summary* file could get messed up, and you would never know. If you do not want to link your workbooks, you can either retype the information or use the Paste Special feature. First, copy the information that you want to transfer. Then click on the cell or area where you want to place that information. Select **Edit** and then **Paste Special**. A dialog box will open. Select **Values and number formats** and click **OK.** This will transfer only the data but not the formula.

Back to the *Summary* file: in cell A1, type the words "Collection Segment." Below that, in cell A2, type the word "Science" or "500s" or whatever is appropriate for the section of your collection you are analyzing. Type "Number of Items" in cell B1, "Average Pub Date" in cell C1, and "Median Pub Date" in cell D1. To make the headings bold, right-click on the box that identifies row 1, select **Format Cells,** select the **Font** tab, and then click **Bold** and **OK.** Your *Summary* file should now look like figure 5-1.

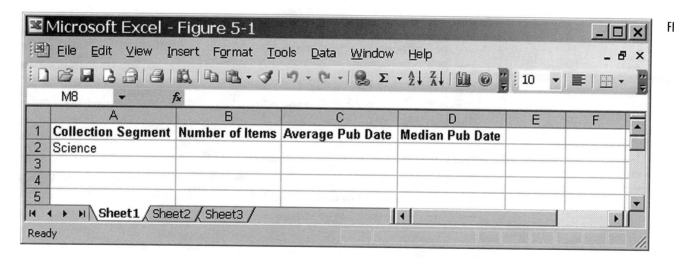

FIGURE 5-1

Collection Size

Now that you have made your decisions and moved some material into other files (where you can repeat these analyses), you are ready to begin studying your circulating collection. Counting the number of items is easy. In your *Working* file, press Ctrl+End and you will go to the last row. The item number of the last row (minus 1 for the row with the column labels) is the number of items in this part of the collection.

Collection Age

In recent years rapid changes in the life sciences and geopolitics have meant that items in those fields can quickly become out of date. In other areas, such as literary criticism and gardening, older materials still have value. Those are easy ones. Now, how about psychology? Have there been major changes in this field? Are the users of your library finding useful material in this part of the collection, or are they walking away because the collection needs updating? A study at the Purdue University Library on how use was affected by item age showed that titles in the Dewey range of 330–339 were regularly used for forty years after publication, while use of titles in the 340–369 range fell off after twenty years, and the 370–379 titles received significant use regardless of their age.[2] (This study was conducted before the use of OPACs, which present the newest items first, so it may no longer be valid.) There are ways of checking on how a collection's age affects use, but before we determine that, we have to find out how old the collection is.

Determining a Collection's Age

The simplest and most common measure of collection age is the average year of publication. Statisticians use the term *mean* instead of average. They do that to be mean. We will stick with *average*. (See chapter 4, "Cleaning Up Data," for reasons publication date is superior to copyright date.) We know you know how to figure averages, but we are going somewhere, so just play along with this next part.

To get the average age of publication, simply add up the years of publication for each item and divide by the number of items. (When analyzing a real collection, you will use the Year column from the material you exported into Excel.) But for this example, say our science section consists of nine volumes. In call number order, they have the following publication dates:

1978

1985

1997

2000

1954

1995

1990

2006

2000

Adding them up, you get 17,905. Divide by 9 (the number of volumes) and you get an average publication date of 1989 (rounding off the fraction). Easy enough to do with a calculator, but your science section actually has hundreds of volumes. Here is how to do it with Excel, using the preceding example of nine volumes.

Step 1. Enter the sample list of dates into an Excel worksheet and click in the cell below the last date (see figure 5-2).

Step 2. Click on **Insert** on the Menu bar and click on **Function** (see figure 5-3). With Excel 2003, you can click on *fx* to the left of the Formula bar as a shortcut to choosing functions without having to click **Insert–Function.**

Step 3. If your version of Excel has a menu of function categories, choose either **All** or **Statistical;** then select the function you want to use (in this case, **Average**) and click **OK** (see figure 5-4).

Step 4. Because you have previously clicked in the cell below the last date, Excel will assume you want to get the average of the column of numbers above where you clicked. After the first time you click **OK,** the formula for figuring an average appears. Click **OK** a second time (or press Enter) and the actual number will be placed in the cell.

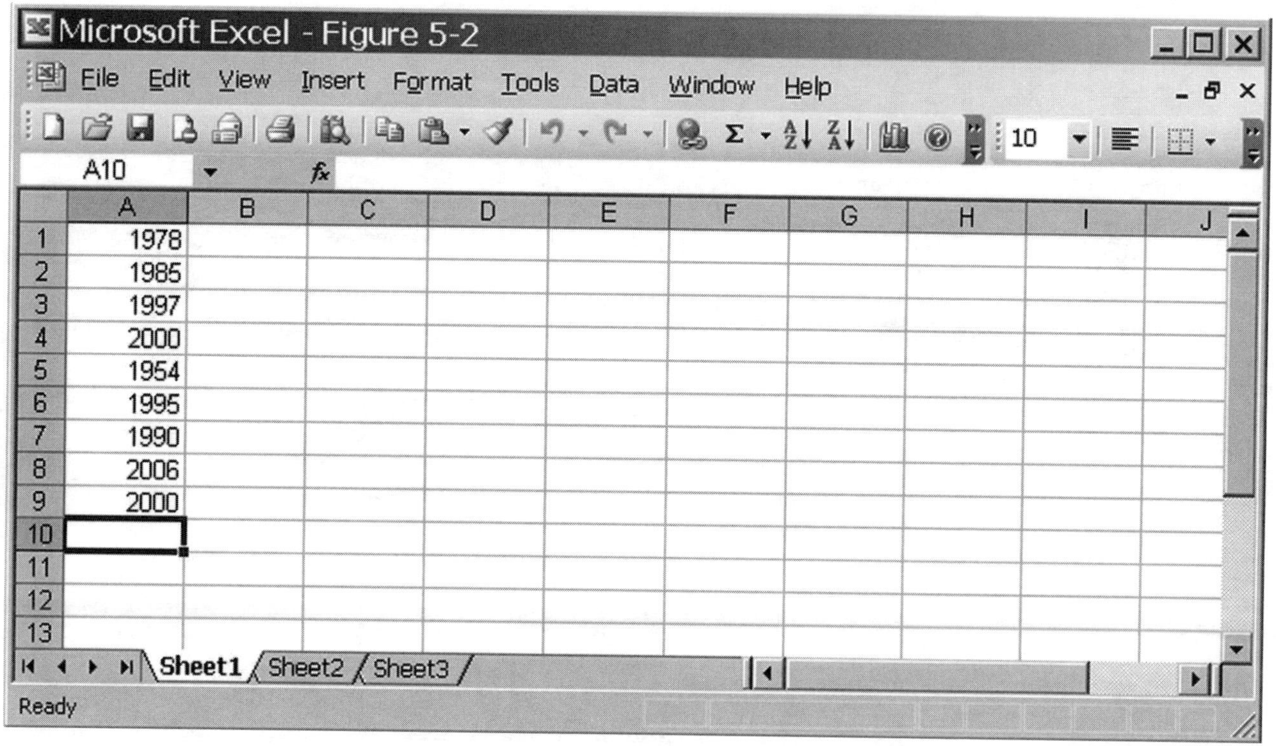
Microsoft Excel - Figure 5-2
File Edit View Insert Format Tools Data Window Help
A10
A B C D E F G H I J
1 1978
2 1985
3 1997
4 2000
5 1954
6 1995
7 1990
8 2006
9 2000
10
11
12
13
Sheet1 Sheet2 Sheet3
Ready

FIGURE 5-2

FIGURE 5-3

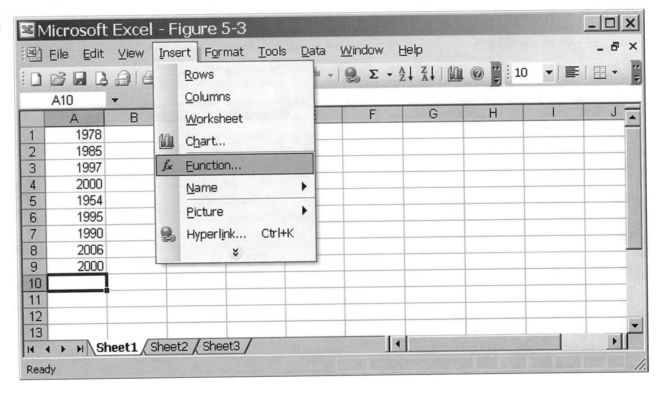

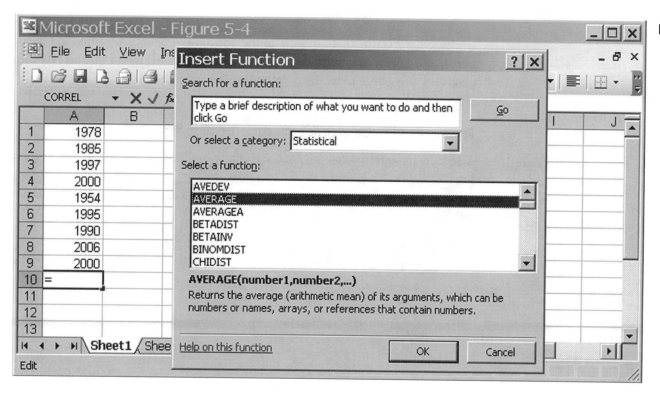

FIGURE 5-4

Now follow these steps with the *Working* file of your actual collection. If the worksheet is so large that scrolling to the bottom is a pain, you can go to the end of the columns by pressing Ctrl+End. Now, in the cell below the last date, use the preceding procedure to let Excel determine the average.

Determining Median Publication Date (the Middle, the 50-50 Point!)

A second measure of age, distinct and often superior to average, is the *median,* the halfway point. Half the books are older, half are younger than the median. If we arrange our example of nine science books by year of publication, we get the following:

1954

1978

1985

1990

1995

1997

2000

2000

2006

To get the median, take the number of items (number of items, not the age of the volumes), in this case 9, and divide by 2, getting 4.5, which rounds up to 5. Count down to the fifth item on the list, and we see that the median age is

1995, a year younger than the average. That 1954 title makes the *average* age of the collection older than the *median* age. Luckily, Excel has a median feature that doesn't require you to sort the collection by publication date.

Look at the little file you created with nine dates typed in it. Using the same list of dates, right-click in the last cell, the one with the average publication date, and select **Clear Contents.** Now, as you did for the average, click on **Insert–Function** on the Menu bar. Select the **Statistical** category, and then select **Median** and click **OK.** Again the formula will appear in the cell. Click **OK** a second time, and the median date will appear. Now, going back to your own data, perform an analysis of the median age in your *Working* file, and record that data in the *Summary* file. These distinctions in determining the age of the collection may seem mostly curiosities for the moment, but when they are paired with collection use, they will be a big help in determining future buying and weeding plans.

Determining an Item's Age

One of the most valuable things Excel can do for you is correlation. Correlation is a statistical comparison of how two things are related. You will learn more about it in chapter 7. A useful correlation for librarians is the relationship between the age of a collection and its use. To perform this correlation, it is necessary to have not just the dates of publication but also the ages of the items in years. To determine each item's age, Excel will subtract the publication age of the item from the current year (or the year in which the data was downloaded). Here is how to do it.

First, in the *Working* file for your real collection (or using the example), insert a column after the Date column. (For a reminder on how to insert a column, see chapter 2.) Label this new column Age. Notice how the other columns moved over, keeping their labels. Now check to see whether all your titles have a number in the Date column. (Click on any individual cell, go to **Data–Sort** on the Menu bar, and tell it to use a **Header row** and sort by **Date.**) If there are any entries that do not have information for Date, they will be grouped together at the bottom. This will probably be a small enough group that you can leave it out of the age calculation and still have statistical validity. To temporarily take the entries out of the mix, insert a new blank row directly under the last item that has a number in the Date column. Now it will be easy to see where to stop.

To have Excel determine the age, you will have it subtract. Click in the cell immediately underneath the label Age (G2 in figure 5-5) to enter the formula for subtraction. To do this, you will need the current year and the cell name of the cell directly under the label Date (F2 in figure 5-5). For example, if you perform this analysis in 2007, then in cell G2 type the equals sign (which tells Excel that it is to perform a formula) and then 2007-F2. (This means subtract the number in cell F2 from 2007.) Your typing will look like this:

=2007-F2

Press Enter and the math is done. Now, click again in the cell where you typed the formula (G2 in the example) and look carefully at that cell. You will notice a small square box in the lower right-hand corner of the cell (see figure 5-5).

Put the mouse directly over the little box until it becomes a plus sign, then click, hold, and drag down to the end of the column (or until the date fields become empty) and release. Excel subtracts the number in all the rows of the Date column from 2007 and fills in the Age column. Save.

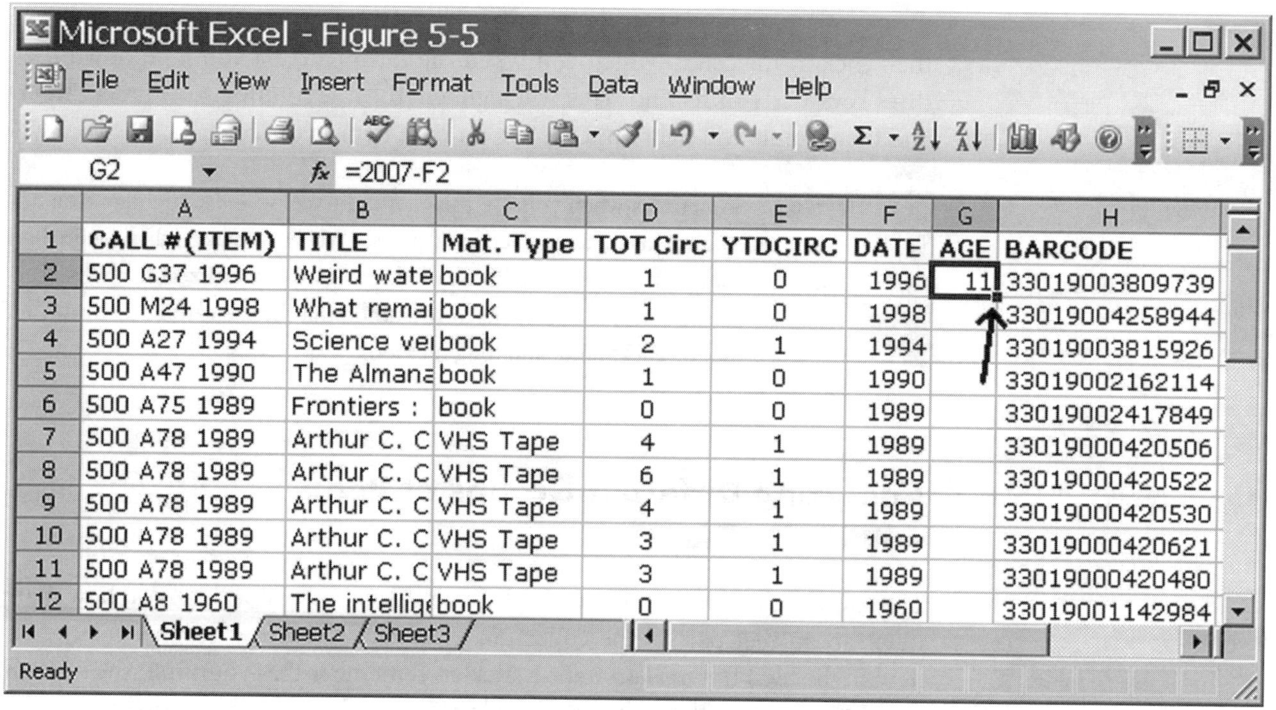

	A	B	C	D	E	F	G	H
1	CALL #(ITEM)	TITLE	Mat. Type	TOT Circ	YTDCIRC	DATE	AGE	BARCODE
2	500 G37 1996	Weird wate	book	1	0	1996	11	33019003809739
3	500 M24 1998	What remai	book	1	0	1998		33019004258944
4	500 A27 1994	Science vei	book	2	1	1994		33019003815926
5	500 A47 1990	The Almana	book	1	0	1990		33019002162114
6	500 A75 1989	Frontiers :	book	0	0	1989		33019002417849
7	500 A78 1989	Arthur C. C	VHS Tape	4	1	1989		33019000420506
8	500 A78 1989	Arthur C. C	VHS Tape	6	1	1989		33019000420522
9	500 A78 1989	Arthur C. C	VHS Tape	4	1	1989		33019000420530
10	500 A78 1989	Arthur C. C	VHS Tape	3	1	1989		33019000420621
11	500 A78 1989	Arthur C. C	VHS Tape	3	1	1989		33019000420480
12	500 A8 1960	The intellig	book	0	0	1960		33019001142984

FIGURE 5-5

If your *Working* file has long columns of data and dragging down is tedious, then click in the cell in which you typed the formula (G2) and hold down these three keys: Ctrl+Shift+End. That will highlight the Age column. Now press Ctrl+D, and the formula will figure out the age for each item in the column.

 WARNING! Sometimes when you use this method Excel will also highlight the next column over, and when you press Ctrl+D it makes changes in both columns. This is one of those maddening aspects of Excel that we warned you about. If this happens to you, undo the change with **Edit–Undo,** and use the click, hold, and drag method.

Analyzing Different Groups of Items within the File

The row number on the left-hand side of your *Working* file will tell you how many items are in that part of the collection. (Just check the row number for the last item in the file.) If you want to be a stickler, remember that your first row is labels, so subtract 1 from the number of the last row, and you have the total number of items. There will be times when you will want to count the number of a certain type of item that is in the bigger file (for example, the number that are DVDs, or the number that were published in the last five years).

To do this count, first sort your data by whatever column you want to count (call number, material type, etc.). Highlight the items you want to count in the column. Right-click on the bar at the bottom of the screen, which has the word Ready on it. Click on **Count** and the total number of items you selected will appear on the Ready bar (see figure 5-6). The Count feature counts cells, so make sure you have highlighted only the cells with your criterion and not adjacent ones as well.

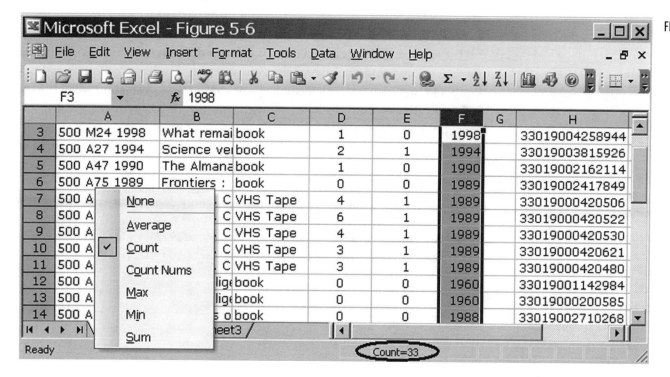

FIGURE 5-6

TIP On a Macintosh, on the Ready bar, click in the box to the left of the letters SCRL. Then you will see your options, one of which is Count.

Compare age for different parts of the collection, and you already have something useful. Because outliers like the odd book from 1869 can distort the average date, we think median is the most useful measure. See chapter 8 for examples of a *Summary* file with data from many parts of the collection.

A useful analysis is to determine the median and average ages of a large section, such as science, and then repeat the process with different subdivisions within that range. You may find that the median age of the entire science collection is 1995, but books on biology have a median age of 1989. That information should shape collection development decisions by itself, but before you start buying, let's get even more information by analyzing the collection's use.

NOTES

1. A 2005 study to see if students preferred print or electronic books when both were available found that format preference depended on the title. See Marilyn Christianson and Marsha Aucoin, "Electronic or Print Books, Which Are Used?" *Library Collections, Acquisitions and Technical Services* 29 (2005): 71–81.
2. Aridaman K. Jain, "A Statistical Study of Book Use" (PhD thesis, Purdue University, 1967), 190–91.

Analyzing Circulation

In use studies, circulation is the name of the game, and your ILS should have a built-in method of recording it. We laid out some reasons for measuring circulation in chapter 1, so we won't repeat them here. By now you have downloaded your data, cleaned it up, made a *Working* file, and started your analysis and *Summary* files. Now it's time to really have some fun. After all that hard work, most of these analyses can be done quickly, perhaps an hour for each file you analyze.

Analysis begins with the raw numbers of how much the collection, or the part of the collection, you are analyzing was used. If you have not yet downloaded circulation data from your own collection, you can use the sample file found at http://www.ala.org/editions/extras/Greiner09331/.

Circulation Numbers

To determine the total circulation, you will need to add the numbers in that column. Excel makes it easy. Scroll to the end of the Total Circulation column. (If it is long, an easy way to get to the bottom of your spreadsheet is to press Ctrl+End. Ctrl+Home takes you to the top.) Click in the cell immediately below the last row, and then, in the toolbar, click twice on the sigma (Σ) button (see figure 6-1). The first time you click, it will show the formula; the second time, it gives you the answer. This is your total circulation for this part of the collection. Do this for the Current Year Circ. and Last Year Circ. and enter that information in your *Summary* file, creating new column headings as needed.

FIGURE 6-1

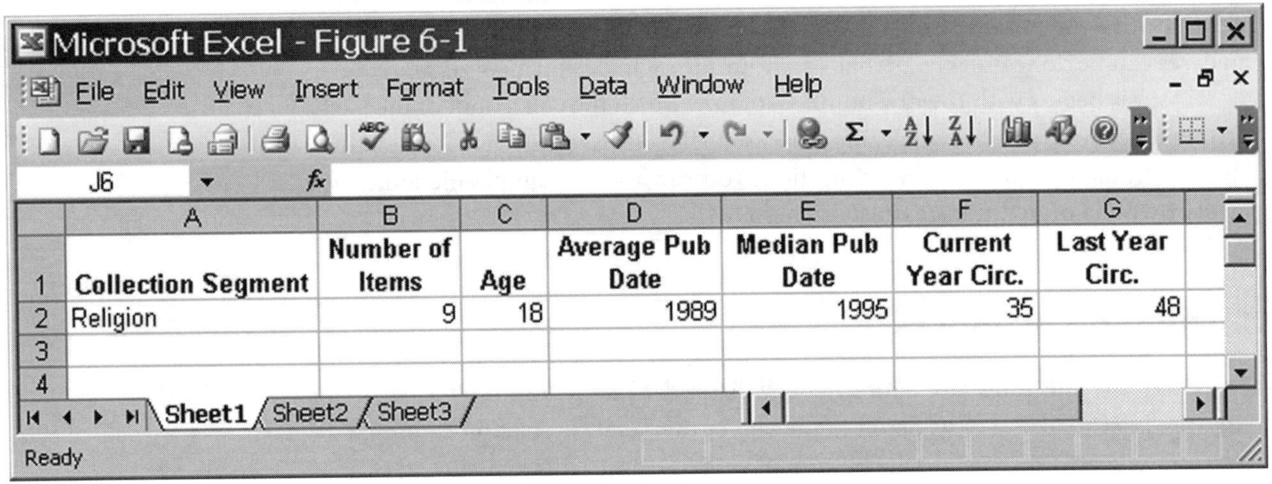

Microsoft Excel - Figure 6-1

File Edit View Insert Format Tools Data Window Help

J6

Collection Segment	Number of Items	Age	Average Pub Date	Median Pub Date	Current Year Circ.	Last Year Circ.	
Religion	9	18	1989	1995	35	48	

Sheet1 / Sheet2 / Sheet3 /

Ready

Average Use per Title (Turnover)

Average use not only shows typical use of this part of the collection, but as we shall see, it is the best predictor of future use. You have already entered the sums of the circulation columns into your *Summary* file, so now go back to the *Working* file and clear the cells that recorded the total number in the column (right-click and select **Clear Contents**). Click again in the now-empty cell to alert Excel that you will be doing something with the column above. To determine the average, click on *fx* (or choose **Insert–Function** from the Menu bar), select **Statistical,** and then select **Average,** just as you did for age in the preceding chapter (see figure 6-2). Press Enter twice to have the average use number placed in the cell.

Switch to your *Summary* file, create the necessary column, and enter this data. Now, if you want, you can determine the median use and again record it in the *Summary.*

Past Use Is the Best Predictor of Future Use

A very good reason to study use is that it is the best indicator of future use of your collection. This is true in academic and public libraries. More complicated methods of predicting future use have been suggested, but Terrence Brooks has shown that neither Autoregressive Integrated Moving Average (ARIMA) nor Straight Line Regression analyses predicted future use any better than did simple averages for monthly and yearly circulation.[1] Of course, that is assuming no changes are made in the collection. Part of the message of this book is that libraries should change their collection in response to customer demand, and this, of course, will change use.

FIGURE 6-2

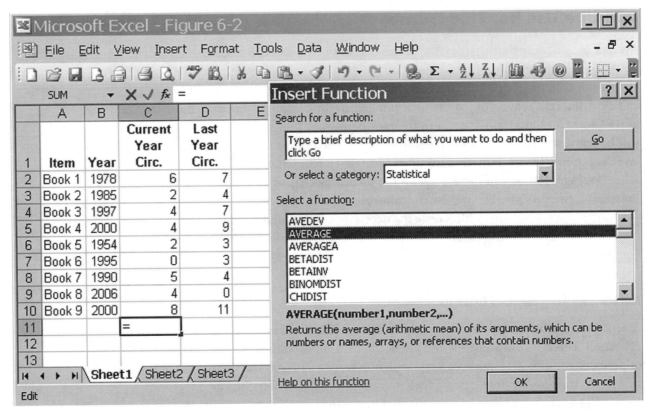

Number and Percentage of Items Checked Out or Unavailable

Shelf bias, or collection bias, is the concept that, for patrons, a library's collection is not what is owned but what is on the shelves. *Shelf bias* means that the most popular items (which are usually checked out) are not what your patrons have available to them. Rather, they see and have access to only those less-popular books that remain on the shelf.[2] An item is unavailable to a patron either because it is checked out or because it has some other status such as "in repair." It is useful to know how much of your collection is in use at a given time and how much is unavailable for other reasons.

The Circulation Status column of your *Working* file is the tool to determine availability. This analysis is best done in two parts: unavailable because the item is checked out, and unavailable for any other reason. If you removed unavailable items from this file for another analysis, it is time to return them. Sort your data by the Circulation Status column. (For information on how to sort, see chapter 2.) After the sort, the "available" books will be together, by whatever code your ILS uses, and you will also have groupings of the unavailable items. Find the items that have the status "checked out." Count them with the process you learned in chapter 5.

Now that you have your count, create a column in your *Summary* file called Number of Items Checked Out and enter the data. Still in the *Summary* file, label the next column Percentage of Items Checked Out and use a calculator to divide the number of checked-out items by the total number of items in your *Working* file. You will get a decimal number, such as .11054. Move the decimal point over two places, and you learn (in this example) that 11 percent of this part of the collection was checked out on the day you ran the data. (Excel can figure percentages for you as well. Instructions on how to do that are found in chapter 8.)

> There are 70 million books in American libraries, but the one I want to read is always out.
>
> —Tom Masson (1866–1934)

Number and Percentage of Items
Unavailable but Not Checked Out

You can repeat this process for the total number of items unavailable for any reason other than "checked out," such as "bindery," "missing," or "in repair." If theft is a problem at your institution, you can figure out the number of missing items by themselves. Do what is right for your institution. After you analyze your entire collection, information about the number and percentage of items in use, or unavailable because of library procedures, or just plain missing will be useful in making decisions about security, workload in technical services, and perhaps budget allocation.

Number and Percentage of Collection Used
in the Last Year (or Two Years)

A 1911 study of the Grand Rapids (Michigan) Public Library looked at what percentage of books in each Dewey Decade were not used over a three-year period. Answers ranged from 28 percent of the 300s to only 8 percent of the 400s receiving no use.[3] This study didn't measure how many times an item was used, but it did reveal how many items were "active." To find this information for your collection, sort the *Working* file by the date of last circulation. The Checkout dates will now be in chronological order. Find the items that were checked out on the day you downloaded the data, then scroll through the Last Circulation column until you find the items that were checked out a year before. Count the cells using the method described previously and record the number in your *Summary* file. Then divide this number by the total number of items in the collection, and you will see what percentage was used at least once. One more column for the ol' *Summary* file.

You can repeat this process to see the number and percentage of items in your collection used at least once in the last month, two years, three years, and so on. This information will be useful when it comes time to weed or to see how lively a particular range is. After you have grouped the items that circulated in the time period, insert a blank row under the last item in the list and a blank row before the first item in the list, and then determine the average and median ages for those items that circulated during this period.[4] Be sure to delete those blank rows when you are done.

Items Added in the Past Year

To determine the number of items added in the past year (the year you are analyzing), sort the *Working* file by Catalog or Publication Date, and count the number with the most recent year. Repeat this process for the past five years (or whatever number seems right for your collection), and record these in your *Summary* file. While you have them sorted, insert a row beneath the last row with this data. Now use the sigma (Σ) button to add the circulation for these more recent items. Create a column in the *Summary* file and record that data as well. Then delete the row you inserted.

Circulation to Acquisitions Ratio

While you have the number of items that circulated last year, and the number added last year, determine the Circulation to Acquisitions ratio.[5] This ratio shows the relationship between use for all items in this part of the collection and the number of new items added to it. The ratio is determined by dividing the number of items that circulated in the past year by the number of items added to that part of the collection.

Continue on this line by measuring the proportion of each area's new titles that circulated in the first year of ownership.[6] You will divide the number of new items that circulated by the number of new items to get a percentage. To do this with Excel, find the column with the publishing date or, better, the cataloging date or, best (if available), the date the item was placed on the shelf. Excel can do this in a two-part sort.

Step 1. Click on a single cell in the file and select **Data–Sort** from the Menu bar. From the Sort by drop-down menu, choose **Catalog date,** and in the Then by menu, choose **Circulation Date** (or **Last Checkin,** or whatever label you used). Click **OK.**

Step 2. Look in the Date column to find and record the number of books that were cataloged last year. The advantage of the second-level sort now becomes apparent, because all the items you just counted that had a use in the past year will be grouped together.

Step 3. Count that number, divide the number that were used by the total number added, and figure your percentage.

Step 4. Record the raw numbers and percentages in the *Summary* file.

Use by Type of Material

This analysis will inform you about how much your patrons use DVDs, CDs, and other media. In the *Working* file, sort the data by the Material Type column. This gathers books, videos, and DVDs with similar materials. At the beginning and end of each group, insert a blank row by clicking on the row number immediately below the last item of the group, and use the right mouse button to insert a row. Have the rest of the material move down. Now you can repeat any of the preceding analyses for just this material, using the new blank row as a place for Excel to place the numbers.

When you move information about use by material type to the *Summary* file, place it on a new worksheet. Doing so will allow easy comparison of the use of different types of media, and when you want to summarize your data you won't accidentally double count items that were counted both by call number and by material type. To create a new worksheet in your file, right-click on the tab at the bottom of the page and then choose **Insert** and then **Worksheet.** Name it DVD or Audiovisual or whatever. (You can repeat this process as many times as you want.) Copy the column headings from the first page, and remember to save as you go. Folks tend to overlook tabs at the bottom of Excel files and never see them, so you might want to put a note to yourself under the data on the first worksheet of the *Summary* file.

Use by Location

If your library has more than one branch or campus, you can compare circulation by location. (This will require another tab at the bottom of the *Summary* file.) In your *Working* file, sort by Location (as you did for Material Type), and then add a blank row between locations. Now repeat the various analyses you have done before. These analyses will allow you to compare use between each library location and to compare each location's use to that of the collection as a whole.[7] To compare use of a type of material between locations, do a two-level sort: choose **Data–Sort** from the Menu bar, and then sort first by Location and then by Material Type. Now you can compare use of DVDs between locations.

Use by Publisher

Knowing circulation by publisher can be useful for a public library that wants to see if titles from one mystery imprint or romance publisher circulate better than others. Academic libraries that want to assess standing order plans from a publisher can do this as well. Sort your data by Publisher, insert a blank row under each group of publishers, and then determine the averages and other relevant data for each. Remember to delete those blank rows when you are done.

Interlibrary Loan

If your interlibrary loan (ILL) borrowing records can be sorted into call number order, it might (we say might) be useful to analyze ILL borrowing for a range. Ask yourself this question: if the items obtained by ILL had been in our collection, what percentage of the circulation would they have represented? (For example, if this part of your collection had thirty circulations, and you borrowed five items via ILL, then there were a total of thirty-five circulations. Five is 14 percent of thirty-five, so you can say that 14 percent of this range's use came from outside your collection.) Like many of these numbers, analysis of ILL use will gain relevance only when compared to other parts of the collection.

Gathering the data for ILL analysis is time-consuming, especially if borrowed materials use a different classification system than your library uses. More to the point, a study of 16,000 ILL transactions in Illinois libraries found that heavy ILL use for a classification range corresponded to heavy local use, and light local use corresponded to light ILL use.[8] So there may not be a reason to track and measure ILL borrowing by call number, as your own use will tell you where you need more material. This is an old study, however, and the advent of big cooperatives and shared catalogs may mean this information is out of date.

Comparing which items were lent to other libraries for their local use may be even less useful. The University of Pittsburgh study found that 99 percent of items lent out were also used by the library's own patrons.[9] This is an old study, but we haven't seen any updates in our research.

Internal Use

We are putting internal use at the end of this chapter because you might decide not to analyze it. An accurate record of internal use can be valuable, especially for noncirculating materials, but there are two difficulties you will need to overcome before internal use will be a meaningful statistic. You may decide it isn't worth the effort, because getting *meaningful* internal use figures means getting your staff to do things consistently.

The first difficulty is simply defining what constitutes an internal use. It can be any combination of the following: picked up off a table after patrons have left, found grossly misshelved (implying that a patron put it back on any old shelf after using it), misshelved in any manner, lying on a bookshelf near its proper place, lying on a staff member's desk, used by a reference librarian to answer a question, or used by a librarian in a failed attempt to answer a question. Pick a combination of definitions, and stick to it. By being consistent, you will be able to track changes over time, which is the main thing.

You will also need to check whether and how your ILS records internal use. Does it automatically add internal use to circulation or does it record it separately? Is a different procedure needed to record internal use as opposed to checking in from circulation? There is at least one library system (Innovative's Millennium) that records internal use with a distinct check-in method, but doesn't assign a date to that use, reducing the information's utility.

The second problem with internal use is more difficult to solve. After defining internal use, you need to train the staff to apply the definition and follow whatever process is needed to record internal use, and to do so consistently. You will also need signage to encourage patrons not to "help out" by reshelving materials themselves. Good luck. Even in libraries with clear definitions and procedures, we have seen circulation managers record internal use on anything that showed the least indication that someone touched it, in order to "get our numbers up," and we have seen circulation workers reshelve materials directly because they didn't want to bother with the check-in effort. If you don't think you can implement a reasonably accurate internal use method, we suggest not doing it at all.

There is also research from 1979 that supports the idea that, in academic libraries, internal use is strongly equated with circulating use.[10] If that is still true, gathering internal use statistics may not be necessary anyway. Still, it remains the only way we have to record use of noncirculating materials, aside from marking them on an inside cover.

Effect of Online Resources on Use

Librarians may wonder how a subscription to online resources will affect the use of print materials. They may even decide to reduce a print budget in an area that has a newly purchased electronic counterpart. One of the values of a use study is that it will show if print use is affected by electronic information sources. Say a library subscribes to an auto-repair database. Use of repair guides may drop, but it may not—it could be that the electronic version reaches an audience that did not use the print version, and the users of those beautifully grimy Chilton's manuals continue to favor print. If you do a yearly analysis, compare use from year to year, especially before and after the subscription to the electronic resource. You might be able to trim your print budget, but you might not. The best part is, you don't have to guess—a use study will tell you!

Other Uses

It should be clear that this data can be run any number of ways. It is possible that other combinations and comparisons could be interesting as well. One of these, correlation, is covered in chapter 7. Chapter 8 will tell you how to use your completed *Summary* file to gain even more insights into your collection.

NOTES

1. Terrence A. Brooks, "Naïve vs. Sophisticated Methods of Forecasting Public Library Circulation," *Library and Information Science Research* 6, no. 2 (April–June 1984): 205–14. The study of circulation as a predictor of use in academic libraries is Herman H. Fussler and Julian L. Simon, *Patterns of Use of Books in Large Research Libraries* (Chicago: University of Chicago Press, 1969), cited in Sharon Baker and F. Wilfrid Lancaster, *The Measurement and Evaluation of Library Services*, 2nd ed. (Arlington, VA: Information Resources Press, 1991), 82.

2. Michael K. Buckland, *Book Availability and the Library User* (New York: Pergamon Press, 1975), 93–97.

3. S. H. Ranck, "The Problem of the Unused Book," *Library Journal* 36 (1911): 428–29, cited in Aridaman K. Jain, "A Statistical Study of Book Use" (PhD thesis, Purdue University, 1967), 130–31.

4. Karen Krueger, *Coordinated Cooperative Collection Development for Illinois Libraries* (Springfield: Illinois State Library, 1983), 107.

5. Marilyn Levine, "The Circulation/Acquisition Ratio: An Input-Output Measure for Libraries," *Information Processing and Management* 16, no. 6 (June 1980): 313–15, cited in Mike Day and Don Revill, "Towards the Active Collection: The Use of Circulation Analysis in Collection Evaluation," *Journal of Librarianship and Information Science* 27, no. 3 (1995): 150.

6. Day and Revill, "Towards the Active Collection."

7. For an interesting 1966 study comparing use by Dewey area between the Toledo (Ohio) Central Library and one of its branches, read E. E. Moon's editorial "Dewey Proportions," *Library Journal* 91 (June 1, 1966): 2783. Moon presents a lot of detail from a study made by Robert Franklin.

8. W. Aguilar, "The Application of Relative Use and Interlibrary Demand in Collection Development," *Collection Management* 8, no. 1 (1986): 15–24, cited in F. W. Lancaster and Beth Sandore, *Technology and Management in Library and Information*

Services (Champaign: University of Illinois Graduate School of Library and Information Sciences, 1997), 72.

9. Allen Kent et al., *Use of Library Materials: The University of Pittsburgh Study* (New York: Marcel Dekker, 1979), 10.

10. Ibid., 26. The Pittsburgh study found that 79 percent of items that had an "internal use" (counted as being picked up off a table or shelving cart) also had at least one external circulation.

Chapter 7

Correlation and Its Uses

The race is not always to the swift, nor the battle to the strong, but that's the way to bet.

—Damon Runyon

We know it from experience: new books get more use than old books. We also "just know" that it is more important to have recent materials in the computer software collection than in the religion section. A twenty-year-old book on Tibetan Buddhism may have some life in it, but try getting someone to check out a twenty-year-old computer book. We don't need no stinkin' software to know that. But how about books on psychology? Plumbing? Cooking? When does a collection "get old"? For that, we need to learn the relationship between the age of the books and their use. That relationship is a *correlation* (think of it as "co-relation").

About Correlation

Correlation shows a relationship between two groups of things. For example, there is a relationship between educational achievement and lifetime earnings. Does that mean that everyone with a bachelor of arts degree makes more than every high school dropout? No. But, if we look at the earnings of all the people who didn't graduate from high school and compare them to the earnings of all the people who graduated from college, we can see that there is a relationship between education and earnings. Statisticians have developed a method showing the strength of a relationship between two things—the *correlational coefficient*. The correlational coefficient is a number somewhere between −1.00 and +1.00. If two different groups of information have absolutely no relationship at all (say, the population of New Hampshire and the orbit of Jupiter), the correlational coefficient is zero. Zero means no relationship.

Now, let's say you live in a state with a 5 percent sales tax, and that tax is applied to all purchases. If you buy $100 of library paste, you will be taxed an additional $5, for a total of $105. If you buy $200 of RFID tags, you will be taxed an additional $10, for a total of $210, and so on. The relationship between your purchases and your taxes is perfectly consistent: no matter how much or how little you spend, an additional 5 percent goes to taxes. Because your taxes go up as your purchases go up, this is a *positive* correlation, and because this correlation is absolutely consistent, the correlational coefficient is +1.00.

WARNING! It is important to remember that a positive correlation doesn't necessarily mean a good relationship. It simply means that as one thing increases (spending) so does the other thing (taxes). There is a positive correlation between the amount of candy you eat and the size of your waistline, but no one thinks that is good.

Negative correlations (also known as "inverse relationships") also exist. Compare an athlete's speed as a runner with the likelihood of winning a race. The coach knows that, generally, Ms. Rodriguez takes one minute to run a lap, whereas Ms. Tortuga takes two. Ms. Rodriguez is much more likely to win a race between the two. Here the relationship is negative: the less time it takes the athlete to run a lap, the more likely she is to be a winner. If Ms. Rodriguez *always* had the lowest time in her practice laps and *always* won the race, the correlational coefficient showing the relationship of her lap time to the likelihood of her winning a race would be –1.00 (negative one). This would be a perfect inverse relationship. Just as a positive correlation doesn't mean good, a negative one doesn't mean bad. It just means that as one of the numbers goes down (time per lap) the other goes up (likelihood of winning).

In correlation, as in love, perfect relationships are rare. Sometimes the faster runner stumbles and a slower contestant wins the race. The relationship between speed and victory is not a perfect one. In these cases (and almost always in practice), the correlational coefficient is expressed as a decimal number.

The faster athlete usually wins the race, but occasionally doesn't. The correlation between lap time and victory might really be –0.91. Some lucky souls can eat a lot of candy without seeing their waistline grow. The correlation between candy consumption and waistline expansion might really be +0.65. What do the numbers mean? Think in thirds. If the correlational coefficient is between –0.33 and +0.33, there is no real relationship between the two items. If the correlation is between (plus or minus) 0.34 and 0.65, it is moderately related. If it is higher than (again, plus or minus) 0.66, it is strongly related. (However, we don't recommend telling your spouse that you've figured your relationship as a –0.87.)

Stephen Hawking says that his publishers told him that for every formula he included in his book *A Brief History of Time,* sales would drop by half. The sales of the book you are reading are going to be so small that we can't afford to lose any, so we are not including the formula, which would scare your pants off. You can look it up in any book on statistics, and be glad that Excel can do it for you.

Using Excel to Determine Correlation

You can use the correlational coefficient to see how the age of the collection affects use, and how much. The files you downloaded from your ILS, or the sample available on the website, have the publication date and current year circulation numbers for each item in that part of the collection. (You want to use current year use rather than total use, because total use took place over a series of years, during which the book aged.) The important questions are these: Is the age of the collection affecting circulation today? Are the older books dragging down use?

In chapter 5 you created a column to show the age of the item, not just the publication date. We will use that column now to correlate the age of the items to their use in the current (or most recent) year. If you have *reliable* internal use figures for the past year, you can create a Total Use column and use that one instead. (See chapter 6 on problems of internal use.)

Before you run the correlation, it is necessary to have data in all the cells of both columns of your *Working* file. In the file, locate the columns for Age and Current Year Circulation. It is possible that some items will not have any information for the publication year and age. (A zero is information. A dash or a blank cell is not.) Items without information in either of the columns must be pulled out before the correlation can be run. Sort the *Working* file by Age. Find any rows that have blank cells in the Age column, and cut them out and paste them a few rows under the rest of the data. (You'll put them back when you are done.) Then go back and delete any blank rows (highlight the row, right-click, and choose **Delete**). Repeat this process if there are any items missing use data. (Remember, zero is data.)

If your collection has many items that have been unavailable for a long time (see chapter 6), sort by circulation status, and again cut out any item that has a status of anything *except* "available" and "checked out." (In other words, cut out "bindery," "mending," "missing," etc.) Items long missing will have a circulation of zero and may mess up the analysis of how the available collection was used. Tuck those missing items somewhere at the end of the main file, and again close up the data. Now you are ready to correlate.

To find the correlation, follow these steps.

Step 1. Click in an empty cell somewhere below the data (one of the cells between the main file and the items you cut out and pasted below). Excel will place the correlational coefficient in this cell.

Step 2. Click on **Insert–Function,** choose **Statistical** and then **Correl.**

Step 3. Click **OK.** A pop-up will appear, asking which items you want to correlate. Here you will be using the *cell names* that were presented in chapter 2. (It isn't necessary to have the columns you are correlating side by side—we did it in our example for clarity.)

Step 4. In our example (figure 7-1), the cell names that have Current Year Circulation figures are C2 to C10. So, in the field for Array 1, you would type C2:C10. (The colon is necessary, and do not put in a space.) For Array 2, type D2:D10, for Age.

Step 5. Click **OK;** Excel figures the correlational coefficient and puts it in the cell you designated. In the example it is –0.734916492, or –0.73. It is a negative number because the younger an item is, the more likely it is to be used. The –0.73 means that there is a strong correlation between age and circulation.

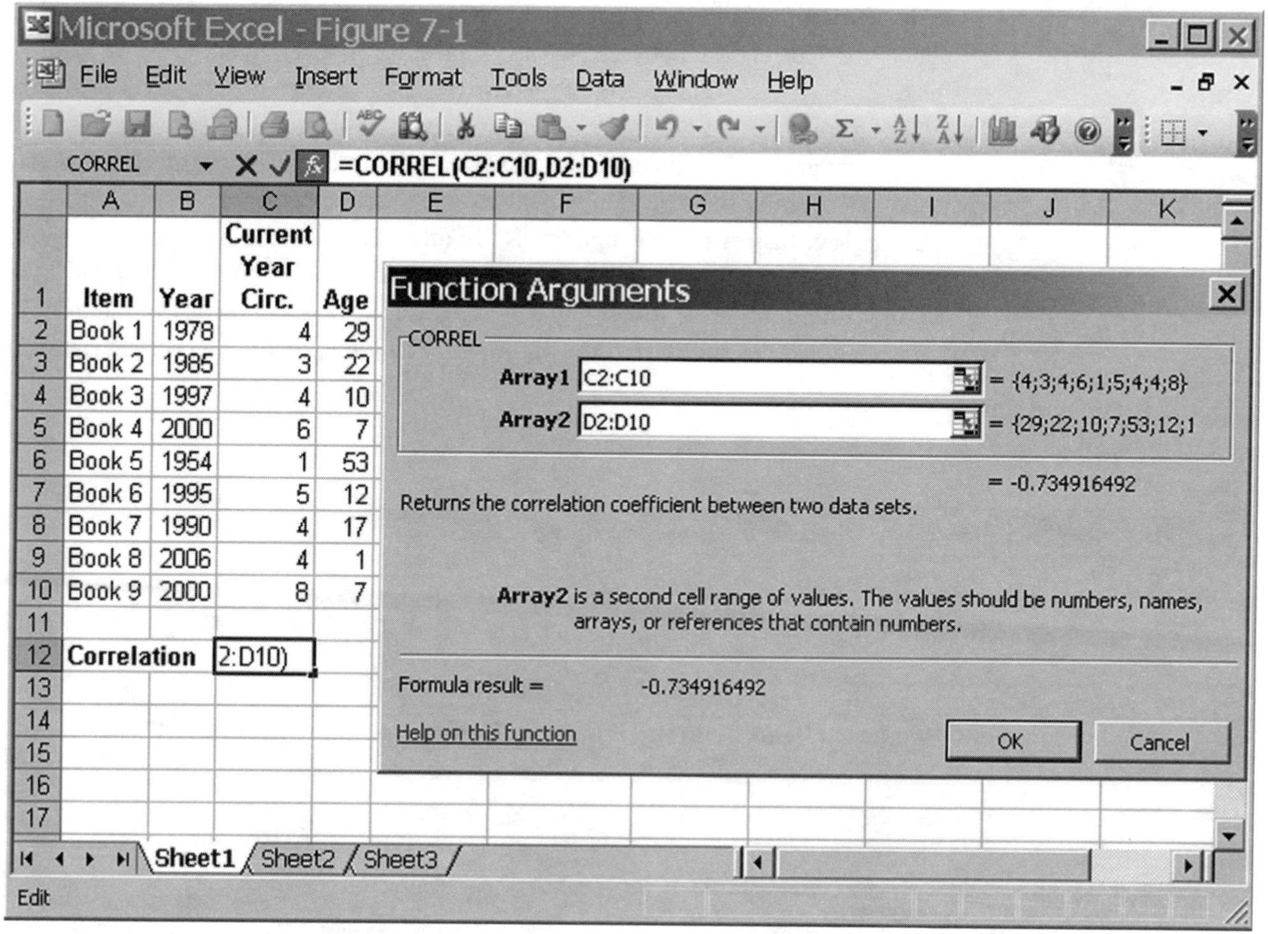
Microsoft Excel - Figure 7-1
File Edit View Insert Format Tools Data Window Help
CORREL
=CORREL(C2:C10,D2:D10)
A B C D E F G H I J K
1 Item Year Current Year Circ. Age
2 Book 1 1978 4 29
3 Book 2 1985 3 22
4 Book 3 1997 4 10
5 Book 4 2000 6 7
6 Book 5 1954 1 53
7 Book 6 1995 5 12
8 Book 7 1990 4 17
9 Book 8 2006 4 1
10 Book 9 2000 8 7
11
12 Correlation 2:D10)
13
14
15
16
17
Sheet1 Sheet2 Sheet3
Edit
Function Arguments
CORREL
Array1 C2:C10 = {4;3;4;6;1;5;4;4;8}
Array2 D2:D10 = {29;22;10;7;53;12;1
= -0.734916492
Returns the correlation coefficient between two data sets.
Array2 is a second cell range of values. The values should be numbers, names, arrays, or references that contain numbers.
Formula result = -0.734916492
Help on this function
OK
Cancel

FIGURE 7-1

If you do this for your collection, create a column in the *Summary* file with a label like Correlation between Age and Current Year Use. (Well, really something like Corr Age/CY Use.) Type in the correlational coefficient that Excel provided (see figure 7-2).

Now go back to the *Working* file, clear the cell that has your correlational coefficient, and delete the blank rows between the parts of your collection that have use and age figures and the other parts. (In other words, make it one long file again, without any spacing rows.) Now you can sort by call number or whatever and have everything in order. If something gets messed up, you have the *Clean* file to start fresh, and you've transferred the findings to the *Summary* file, so nothing is lost.

FIGURE 7-2

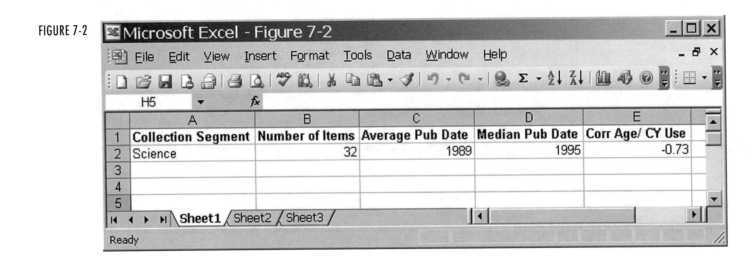

	A	B	C	D	E
1	Collection Segment	Number of Items	Average Pub Date	Median Pub Date	Corr Age/ CY Use
2	Science	32	1989	1995	-0.73
3					
4					
5					

Now that you have determined the correlation between age and use in the various parts of your collection, what do you do with that information?

Applying Correlation to Your Library

You can use the correlational coefficient to help budget money in your collection areas, especially in tight times. Say that at the end of the fiscal year, you ran the correlation to age and recent use (combined circulation for the current year and the year before), and got the following correlations for each of these Dewey groups:

000–099	–0.75
100–199	–0.29
200–299	+0.12
300–399	–0.45
400–499	–0.52
500–599	–0.66
600–699	–0.64
700–799	–0.20
800–899	+0.22
900–999	–0.44

Remember, negative numbers mean that younger titles (those with a lower age) got more use in the past two years. There is a strong relationship to age and use in the 000–099 range. Patrons have shown a preference for new books in this area.

There is a moderate age/use relationship in the 300s, 400s, 600s, and 900s. These collections would benefit from some refreshing, but patrons don't completely rely on new materials. For the other parts of the collection, new materials don't seem to be important (at least at the time this correlation was run—at some point that may no longer be true). The positive numbers in the 200s and 800s might imply that for these areas older books are preferred, but the coefficient number is too low to confirm that. It is better to say that, for these parts of the collection, older books are used as much as younger ones.[1]

So?

So, when you allocate your collection dollars, you should consider budgeting enough in the 000–099 range to allow for the purchase of a significant amount of new material. The areas with a moderate relationship should get some scratch as well. If you are in a pinch, you could budget just a maintenance amount to the other areas. But be careful! Using a correlation study of age to recent use without considering other factors is a gross simplification, and one that could cause problems later on. Chapter 8 will show you how to tie all your analyses together.

For some collections, a range of 100 Dewey numbers or a major LC classification may be too large to be meaningful. Depending on your library, you may be safe looking at some parts of the collection in big chunks (the 200s—religion), but other areas may need an analysis of smaller subdivisions. If you put all your computer software books together, do them by themselves. You might want to do your travel section as a chunk or break it down into United States and foreign or some other subdivision. The subdivisions you choose will depend on the size, mission, and clientele of your library. You must have at least thirty items in an area for correlation to be statistically valid.

A Bit about Statistical Language

If you find yourself reading an article with correlational formulas in it, the symbol for the correlational coefficient is r (lowercase and italicized). You also might find the phrase "statistical significance." This is a number that is used when only *part* of a set of information, the "statistical sample," is used in an analysis. Statistical significance informs the reader how likely it is that the sample reflects the whole. Because our technique uses the entire collection (or close to it), we don't need to worry about statistical significance. If you want to learn more, we recommend Arthur Hafner's *Descriptive Statistical Techniques for Librarians*.

Uses for Correlational Coefficients

Before we leave this chapter, we should mention three areas where calculating correlations could provide useful information: (1) correlation of age to use for items in the collection that were used in the past year (or two years); (2) correlation of age to use for certain material types (do videos "get old" before books?); and (3) correlation of age to use for serials (if you track serials use by item, finding the age at which issues of a journal are little read may help with storage and weeding decisions). You might be able to think of other applications.

NOTE

1. For an example of a study of how age affected use in an Indian library, see M. S. Sridhar, *Library Use and User Research: With 20 Case Studies* (New Delhi: Concept Publishing, 2002), 155–58.

Chapter 8

The Summary File

Chapters 5, 6, and 7 showed various ways of looking at collections and use, and how to use Excel to do the calculations. You also set up a *Summary* file, in which you recorded your findings for each section of the collection. The *Summary* file, which gives you a look at all the parts of the collection at once, is the most useful tool in collection analysis. The previous chapters presented a number of ways to crunch the numbers, and if you ran all of them, you might just drown in data. The sample *Summary* file used in this chapter shows a few of the analyses. Use whichever of these analyses make sense for your collection and library.

The sample *Summary* file (see figure 8-1) is the result of an analysis of the circulating collection of a college library at the end of its fiscal year, June 2006. Excluded from the analysis were maps, a few publications such as the college literary magazine, and the "new readers" collection that targets ESL and adult literacy students. To reduce the width of column headings, we formatted the heading row so that the text would wrap (right-click on the row, choose **Format Cells,** click the **Alignment** tab, and check the box next to **Wrap text**). The Total Circ column reflects the circulation of all items in the analysis since the library changed its ILS midway through 1999. For ease of presentation, the collection is arranged by large call number groups. Some Dewey classes were broken into smaller sections to make handling easier and to show that many groupings are possible. In practice, arranging the collection by topics, smaller categories such as Dewey divisions, or budget lines reveals more, but that is too many rows to present easily in this book.

There are a number of interesting things to see here. Median publication dates run from 1977 to 1997. Average circulation per item since 1999 ranges from 1.1 uses per item to 4.4. And there is no real correlation of age to current year use (at least in this broad-level overview). As interesting as it is, this information can be more useful if we determine use for the whole collection. Begin with the total number of items in the circulating collection. You can follow along using your own *Summary* sheet or download this one from the website http://www.ala.org/editions/extras/Greiner09331/.

FIGURE 8-1

Microsoft Excel - Figure 8-1

File   Edit   View   Insert   Format   Tools   Data   Window   Help

P16

Range	Items	Avg Pub	Med Pub	Total Circ	CY Circ	Items w/ Circ	Avg Circ	# items w/ Circ 05-06	Correl Age / CY Use	Items Pub Last 5 Yrs	Total Circ Items Pub Last 5 Yrs	#02-06 Pubs w/ Circ CY	YTD Circ for 02-06 Items
000-099	3749	1992	1997	8887	1112	2269	2.4	743	-0.20	705	1910	295	523
100-199	4524	1987	1990	11593	2144	3324	2.6	1334	-0.20	381	931	225	456
200-299	2400	1984	1988	5869	925	1659	2.4	630	-0.10	159	411	82	143
300-399	28414	1988	1991	52115	8367	16705	1.8	8367	-0.20	2548	5892	2283	2283
400-499	3644	1986	1988	8962	1461	2317	2.5	849	-0.25	148	421	93	187
500-549	3919	1987	1990	16353	1752	2663	4.2	997	-0.19	241	511	103	226
550-599	3577	1984	1988	8926	1266	2497	2.5	826	-0.18	236	576	102	243
600-615	2887	1992	1995	9657	1661	2131	3.3	913	-0.23	461	1792	255	657
615-625	5829	1991	1993	14673	2353	4002	2.5	1461	-0.23	760	1589	349	677
626-650	4715	1989	1991	8768	1534	3094	1.9	1073	-0.24	606	1013	300	504
651-699	4151	1991	1993	6895	1314	2370	1.6	123	-0.25	529	1102	249	480
700-749	4157	1987	1990	15292	2633	3359	3.7	1491	-0.23	362	1045	209	550
750-799	6813	1988	1991	30292	6672	5279	4.4	2680	-0.05	785	3260	484	1652
800-809	2636	1978	1983	3455	595	1227	1.3	363	-0.21	76	189	39	95
810-815	10093	1981	1986	14733	2257	5210	1.5	1583	-0.15	301	802	138	328
816-849	7320	1974	1977	8316	1262	3190	1.1	905	-0.15	123	326	56	125
850-899	3468	1980	1983	3958	562	1640	1.1	433	0.00	29	42	13	15
900-999	13496	1983	1988	27546	4370	8273	2	2808	-0.20	1069	2542	515	1071

Sheet1 / Sheet2 / Sheet3

Ready

Total Number of Items

In the first row under the cell with 900–999, type the word TOTALS (A20 in the example; see figure 8-2). Click in the cell under the column labeled Items (number of items), and add, following the directions in chapter 6. If you get something odd looking, you need to widen the column so the full number fits. Repeat this for Total Circ, CY Circ (Current Year Circulation), and the other columns that have raw numbers. Don't do this with Average and Median Publication date—those are weighted inconsistently, depending on the number of items in their subsections. Likewise, skip the Avg Circ and Correl (Correlation) columns. To bring the totals out in a bold font, highlight that TOTALS row by right-clicking on the row number, then choose **Format Cells.** In the dialog box select the **Font** tab and then select **Bold** under **Font style.** Everything in this row will now be in bold print. The *Summary* file should now look like figure 8-2.

FIGURE 8-2

Microsoft Excel - Figure 8-2

File   Edit   View   Insert   Format   Tools   Data   Window   Help

U18

	A	B	C	D	E	F	G	H	I	J	K	L	M	N
1	Range	Items	Avg Pub	Med Pub	Total Circ	CY Circ	Items w/ Circ	Avg Circ	Items w/ Circ 05-06	Correl Age / CY Use	Pub Last 5 Yrs	Total Circ Items Pub Last 5 Yrs	#02-06 Pubs w/ Circ CY	YTD Circ for 02-06 Items
2	000-099	3749	1992	1997	8887	1112	2269	2.4	743	-0.20	705	1910	295	523
3	100-199	4524	1987	1990	11593	2144	3324	2.6	1334	-0.20	381	931	225	456
4	200-299	2400	1984	1988	5869	925	1659	2.4	630	-0.10	159	411	82	143
5	300-399	28414	1988	1991	52115	8367	16705	1.8	8367	-0.20	2548	5892	2283	2283
6	400-499	3644	1986	1988	8962	1461	2317	2.5	849	-0.25	148	421	93	187
7	500-549	3919	1987	1990	16353	1752	2663	4.2	997	-0.19	241	511	103	226
8	550-599	3577	1984	1988	8926	1266	2497	2.5	826	-0.18	236	576	102	243
9	600-615	2887	1992	1995	9657	1661	2131	3.3	913	-0.23	461	1792	255	657
10	615-625	5829	1991	1993	14673	2353	4002	2.5	1461	-0.23	760	1589	349	677
11	626-650	4715	1989	1991	8768	1534	3094	1.9	1073	-0.24	606	1013	300	504
12	651-699	4151	1991	1993	6895	1314	2370	1.6	123	-0.25	529	1102	249	480
13	700-749	4157	1987	1990	15292	2633	3359	3.7	1491	-0.23	362	1045	209	550
14	750-799	6813	1988	1991	30292	6672	5279	4.4	2680	-0.05	785	3260	484	1652
15	800-809	2636	1978	1983	3455	595	1227	1.3	363	-0.21	76	189	39	95
16	810-815	10093	1981	1986	14733	2257	5210	1.5	1583	-0.15	301	802	138	328
17	816-849	7320	1974	1977	8316	1262	3190	1.1	905	-0.15	123	326	56	125
18	850-899	3468	1980	1983	3958	562	1640	1.1	433	0.00	29	42	13	15
19	900-999	13496	1983	1988	27546	4370	8273	2	2808	-0.20	1069	2542	515	1071
20	TOTALS	115792			256290	42240	71209		27579		9519	24354	5790	10215

Sheet1 / Sheet2 / Sheet3

Ready

Finding Averages for the Collection as a Whole

Earlier, when you were analyzing parts of the collection where all the items were listed, Excel would determine a column's average by using the *fx* button. With the *Summary* file, it is necessary to use arithmetic, as the columns of figures for Avg Circ are not equally weighted. Determining the average circulation per item for the entire collection (in this case, since 1999) is a good place to start. Find the column labeled Avg Circ. It should have a blank cell in the TOTALS row. One way to get the average is to use a calculator and divide Total Circ by the number of items, and then type in the number. To have Excel do it, and to get comfortable with formulas, do the following:

> Step 1. Click in the blank cell at the bottom of the Avg Circ column, and type the equals sign (remember, this signals Excel to do a calculation).

> Step 2. Type the name of the cell that has the Total Circulation (E20), followed by a slash (/) which means divide, and then the cell number with the total number of items (B20). It should look like this: =E20/B20.

> Step 3. Press Enter, and the average use number for the entire collection will be inserted into the cell.

You might want to format this cell to give you a number after the decimal point. To do so, click on the cell, or highlight the whole column of numbers under Avg Circ. Then right-click and choose **Format Cells.** Choose the **Number** tab, and under the Category heading select **Number.** Then, toggle the Decimal places number to 1. Click **OK.** For average circulation, one decimal place is probably enough, and Excel rounds up if hidden decimal numbers call for it.

Now it is time to find the average circulation of recently published books. Columns K and L have the number of items in the collection for the last five years along with their circulation. Insert a column to the right of column L (Total Circ Items Pub Last 5 Yrs) and label it Avg Circ New Items. (For this example, *new* is defined as being less than five years old.) Here Excel's formula feature is a time-saver. We are going to divide the total circulation of those recent items by the number of recent items for each Dewey range (column L divided by column K). In cell M2, type =L2/K2 and press Enter. Then, repeat the process learned in chapter 5 to drag that formula down the column. (Use the little box.) Go all the way down to the TOTALS row. You may need to format that column to one decimal point. The *Summary* file should now look like figure 8-3.

Now we can see that recent items get higher use than the collection as a whole. This is more eye-opening when we realize that the analysis includes items that have been in the collection for less than five years, which means some of them have been on the shelf for only a month. But, look at the range 500–549. There, the recent books circulated only half as much as the collection as a whole. There has also been a slight drop in the 550–599 range. If librarians were dogs, our ears would prick up. Something is going on here that needs investigating. A couple of possibilities come to mind. One is that the books being purchased don't meet the patrons' needs. However, this is a college, and it is also possible that the increased ease of use of electronic journals has meant less use of print sources. Further thought may lead to other possibilities.

You may be wondering why, if recent books are used more than old ones, this number didn't show up in our correlation of age to use. It is probably due to the low use of the collection in general. The correlation of age to use might be more useful with smaller divisions of the collection or in public library collections that generally receive greater use.

FIGURE 8-3

Microsoft Excel - Figure 8-3

File Edit View Insert Format Tools Data Window Help

M1 · *fx* Avg Circ New Items

	A	B	C	D	E	F	G	H	I	J	K	L	M	N
1	Range	Items	Avg Pub	Med Pub	Total Circ	CY Circ	Items w/ Circ	Avg Circ	Items w/ Circ 05-06	Correl Age / CY Use	Pub Last 5 Yrs	Total Circ Items Pub Last 5 Yrs	Avg Circ New Items	#02-06 Pubs w/ Circ CY
2	000-099	3749	1992	1997	8887	1112	2269	2.4	743	-0.20	705	1910	2.7	295
3	100-199	4524	1987	1990	11593	2144	3324	2.6	1334	-0.20	381	931	2.4	225
4	200-299	2400	1984	1988	5869	925	1659	2.4	630	-0.10	159	411	2.6	82
5	300-399	28414	1988	1991	52115	8367	16705	1.8	8367	-0.20	2548	5892	2.3	2283
6	400-499	3644	1986	1988	8962	1461	2317	2.5	849	-0.25	148	421	2.8	93
7	500-549	3919	1987	1990	16353	1752	2663	4.2	997	-0.19	241	511	2.1	103
8	550-599	3577	1984	1988	8926	1266	2497	2.5	826	-0.18	236	576	2.4	102
9	600-615	2887	1992	1995	9657	1661	2131	3.3	913	-0.23	461	1792	3.9	255
10	615-625	5829	1991	1993	14673	2353	4002	2.5	1461	-0.23	760	1589	2.1	349
11	626-650	4715	1989	1991	8768	1534	3094	1.9	1073	-0.24	606	1013	1.7	300
12	651-699	4151	1991	1993	6895	1314	2370	1.6	123	-0.25	529	1102	2.1	249
13	700-749	4157	1987	1990	15292	2633	3359	3.7	1491	-0.23	362	1045	2.9	209
14	750-799	6813	1988	1991	30292	6672	5279	4.4	2680	-0.05	785	3260	4.2	484
15	800-809	2636	1978	1983	3455	595	1227	1.3	363	-0.21	76	189	2.5	39
16	810-815	10093	1981	1986	14733	2257	5210	1.5	1583	-0.15	301	802	2.7	138
17	816-849	7320	1974	1977	8316	1262	3190	1.1	905	-0.15	123	326	2.7	56
18	850-899	3468	1980	1983	3958	562	1640	1.1	433	0.00	29	42	1.4	13
19	900-999	13496	1983	1988	27546	4370	8273	2.0	2808	-0.20	1069	2542	2.4	515
20	TOTALS	115792			256290	42240	71209	2.2	27579		9519	24354	2.6	5790

Sheet1 / Sheet2 / Sheet3

Ready   Count=20

To go back to the lower use for new materials in the 500s: perhaps the problem in the 500s is not the quality of the materials being purchased, but the quantity. What percentage of the 500s are less than five years old? For that matter, how about the number of recent titles for the library as a whole? Once again, a formula is called for. Insert a column to the right of column K, and label it % of Recent Titles. You will divide the numbers in column K by the numbers in column B. The formula, for cell L2, is =K2/B2*100 (the asterisk is the "times" symbol, × when we were in school). Multiplying by 100 changes the resulting decimal number to a percentage. Use the click, hold, and drag method to repeat the formula for the column, and format the cells to have no decimals—just a whole number (see figure 8-4).

Now we can see that new books form 8 percent of the collection as a whole, and 6 and 7 percent for the ranges of the 500s. It is easy to make the mistake of saying "there are only 1 percent fewer recent books in the 500s" but actually, 7 is 13 percent less than 8, and 6 is 25 percent less. So the problem may be that these collections are getting fewer new books than the whole. Or, maybe those new books are lost in a collection that needs weeding. What percentage of the 500s as a whole has had any use since this library switched to its new system? Repeat the process of determining percentage, in this case inserting a column to the right of column G called % Items w/Circ and dividing column G (Items w/Circ) by column B (Items). Again, multiply by 100 to get a percentage, and format to a whole number (=G2/B2*100, then format cells by number to zero decimal points).

Interesting! The two 500s ranges actually have a higher percentage of items checked out since 1999 than does the collection as a whole. So, comparatively speaking, the 500s are used more than the collection as a whole, but for some reason there has been a drop-off in use of recent books. One more analysis may help. Determine what percentage of new items has been used at least once in the

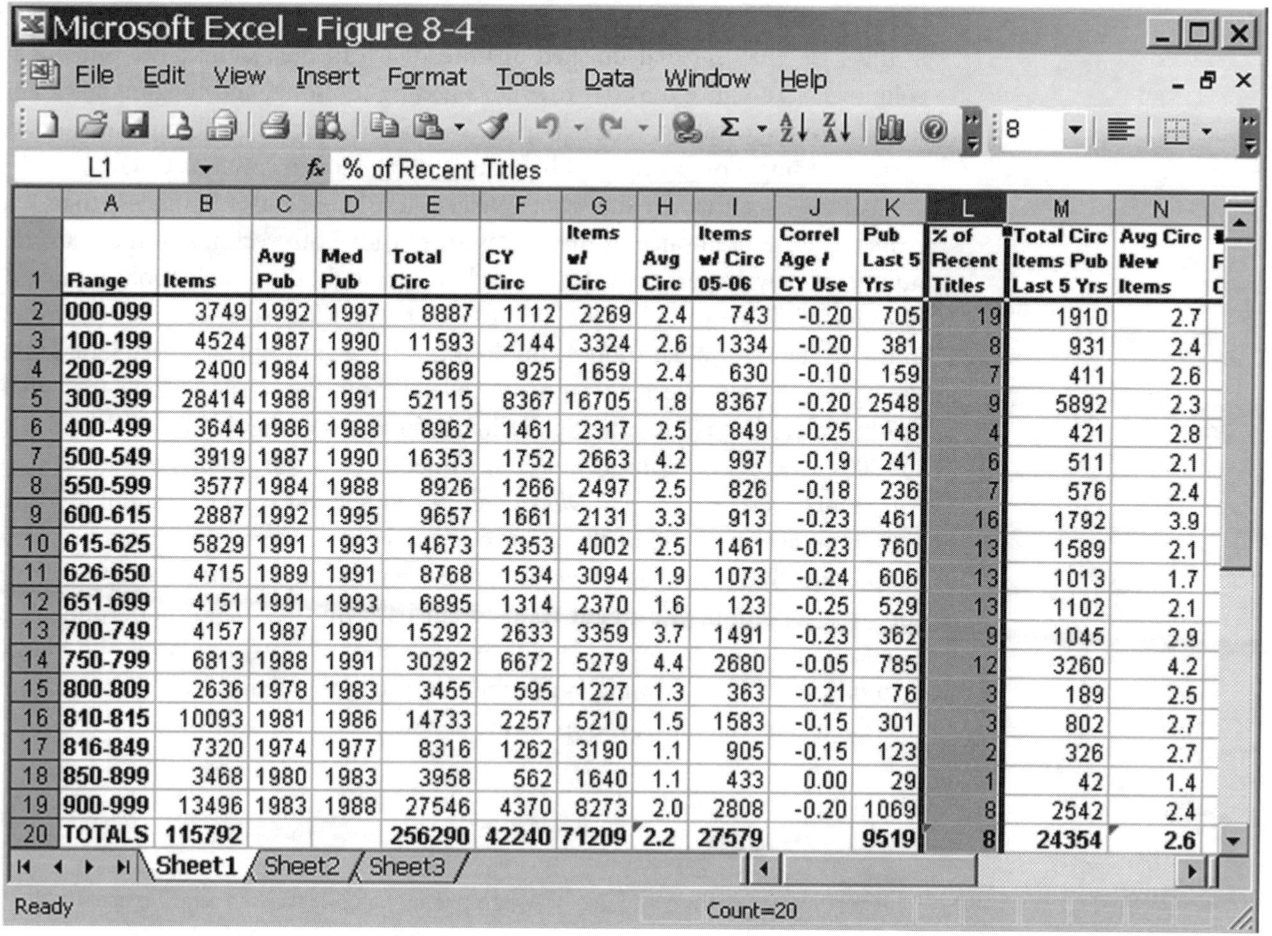

FIGURE 8-4

File Edit View Insert Format Tools Data Window Help

L1   fx % of Recent Titles

	A	B	C	D	E	F	G	H	I	J	K	L	M	N
1	Range	Items	Avg Pub	Med Pub	Total Circ	CY Circ	Items w/ Circ	Avg Circ	Items w/ Circ 05-06	Correl Age / CY Use	Pub Last 5 Yrs	% of Recent Titles	Total Circ Items Pub Last 5 Yrs	Avg Circ New Items
2	000-099	3749	1992	1997	8887	1112	2269	2.4	743	-0.20	705	19	1910	2.7
3	100-199	4524	1987	1990	11593	2144	3324	2.6	1334	-0.20	381	8	931	2.4
4	200-299	2400	1984	1988	5869	925	1659	2.4	630	-0.10	159	7	411	2.6
5	300-399	28414	1988	1991	52115	8367	16705	1.8	8367	-0.20	2548	9	5892	2.3
6	400-499	3644	1986	1988	8962	1461	2317	2.5	849	-0.25	148	4	421	2.8
7	500-549	3919	1987	1990	16353	1752	2663	4.2	997	-0.19	241	6	511	2.1
8	550-599	3577	1984	1988	8926	1266	2497	2.5	826	-0.18	236	7	576	2.4
9	600-615	2887	1992	1995	9657	1661	2131	3.3	913	-0.23	461	16	1792	3.9
10	615-625	5829	1991	1993	14673	2353	4002	2.5	1461	-0.23	760	13	1589	2.1
11	626-650	4715	1989	1991	8768	1534	3094	1.9	1073	-0.24	606	13	1013	1.7
12	651-699	4151	1991	1993	6895	1314	2370	1.6	123	-0.25	529	13	1102	2.1
13	700-749	4157	1987	1990	15292	2633	3359	3.7	1491	-0.23	362	9	1045	2.9
14	750-799	6813	1988	1991	30292	6672	5279	4.4	2680	-0.05	785	12	3260	4.2
15	800-809	2636	1978	1983	3455	595	1227	1.3	363	-0.21	76	3	189	2.5
16	810-815	10093	1981	1986	14733	2257	5210	1.5	1583	-0.15	301	3	802	2.7
17	816-849	7320	1974	1977	8316	1262	3190	1.1	905	-0.15	123	2	326	2.7
18	850-899	3468	1980	1983	3958	562	1640	1.1	433	0.00	29	1	42	1.4
19	900-999	13496	1983	1988	27546	4370	8273	2.0	2808	-0.20	1069	8	2542	2.4
20	TOTALS	115792			256290	42240	71209	2.2	27579		9519	8	24354	2.6

Sheet1 / Sheet2 / Sheet3

Ready   Count=20

last year. That is column P divided by column L (CY stands for Current Year—or in this case, the year that finished in June 2006). In the example, we put this in column R (see figure 8-5). (If the file is getting too long, and toggling back and forth becomes irritating, scrunch up the width of some of the columns you are not currently using. For example, in figure 8-5, we've hidden columns C–G.)

We now see that for the whole collection, 61 percent of items less than five years old were used once in the past year, but for both sections of the 500s, the number is only 43 percent.[1] Maybe this library bought the wrong books in the last few years. Still, we can't be sure, because we haven't looked at usage of electronic journal databases. What should you do if this were your library? First, look at the use figures for your electronic journal collections in the sciences. Have they gone up? Is use higher than in other disciplines? Then look at the shelflist of the titles in the 500s. Are they appropriate for your students? Now start thinking.

Analysis does not tell you what to do! It *can* tell you what you should look at and think about. If use of the science journals has gone up dramatically (or is proportionally higher than other disciplines), and the newer titles look appropriate for your collection, you might want to cut back on the science book budget. If science journal usage doesn't stand out, you might be buying the wrong books. You have the brain, training, and experience. Use the figures to help make your decisions, but remember, you make the decisions.

Relative Use

The best way of comparing use between parts of a collection is relative use. Relative use is the idea that, in a patron-driven collection, a subject area that has 15 percent

FIGURE 8-5

Microsoft Excel - Figure 8-5

File Edit View Insert Format Tools Data Window Help

S20

Range	Items	% Items w/ Circ	Avg Circ	Items w/ Circ 05-06	Age / CY Use	Pub Last 5 Yrs	% of Recent Titles	Total Circ Items Pub Last 5 Yrs	Avg Circ New Items	#02-06 Pubs w/ Circ CY	YTD Circ for 02-06 Items	% New Items Used 2005-06
000-099	3749	61	2.4	743	-0.20	705	19	1910	2.7	295	523	42
100-199	4524	73	2.6	1334	-0.20	381	8	931	2.4	225	456	59
200-299	2400	69	2.4	630	-0.10	159	7	411	2.6	82	143	52
300-399	28414	59	1.8	8367	-0.20	2548	9	5892	2.3	2283	2283	90
400-499	3644	64	2.5	849	-0.25	148	4	421	2.8	93	187	63
500-549	3919	68	4.2	997	-0.19	241	6	511	2.1	103	226	43
550-599	3577	70	2.5	826	-0.18	236	7	576	2.4	102	243	43
600-615	2887	74	3.3	913	-0.23	461	16	1792	3.9	255	657	55
615-625	5829	69	2.5	1461	-0.23	760	13	1589	2.1	349	677	46
626-650	4715	66	1.9	1073	-0.24	606	13	1013	1.7	300	504	50
651-699	4151	57	1.6	123	-0.25	529	13	1102	2.1	249	480	47
700-749	4157	81	3.7	1491	-0.23	362	9	1045	2.9	209	550	58
750-799	6813	77	4.4	2680	-0.05	785	12	3260	4.2	484	1652	62
800-809	2636	47	1.3	363	-0.21	76	3	189	2.5	39	95	51
810-815	10093	52	1.5	1583	-0.15	301	3	802	2.7	138	328	46
816-849	7320	44	1.1	905	-0.15	123	2	326	2.7	56	125	46
850-899	3468	47	1.1	433	0.00	29	1	42	1.4	13	15	45
900-999	13496	61	2.0	2808	-0.20	1069	8	2542	2.4	515	1071	48
TOTALS	115792	61	2.2	27579		9519	8	24354	2.6	5790	10215	61

Sheet1 / Sheet2 / Sheet3

Ready

of the collection's volumes should have about 15 percent of the use (15 divided by 15 is 1, which means use and collection size are balanced). Any area in which the percentage of use is higher than its percentage of the collection should be supported with more items. If the collection size is larger than the use, it needs either weeding or a reduction in new materials or the library may be buying things the patrons don't want (at least, they don't want them as much as more popular areas).

For example, say computer books account for 8 percent of a library's circulation but only 5 percent of the collection. Eight divided by 5 is 1.6, which means the computer book section receives 60 percent more use than an average item in the collection. Likewise, if literary criticism accounts for 6 percent of a collection but only 3 percent of circulation, 3 divided by 6 is 0.5, meaning that books in this collection are used only half the library's average. Patrons who want books from areas with higher-than-average relative use are less likely to find what they need than are patrons of less-popular areas. Buy more books in those areas with high relative use![2]

To figure relative use using Excel, you first need to know the percentage of the collection size and the percentage of use for each section you analyze. Go back to the file in figure 8-5. Our sample collection consists of 115,792 items, which is the sum of column B. The formula is the number of items in each subsection divided by the total collection size, times 100. (The times 100 presents the answer as a percentage, rather than a decimal.) In Excel, insert a column (to the right of B in figure 8-6) and label it % of Coll Size. In the cell for the 000–099 range, type =B2/115792*100 (or whatever cell names fit your own *Summary* file). Use the click, hold, and drag method to repeat the formula for the entire column. Then format the cells in the column to have zero decimal points.

FIGURE 8-6

Microsoft Excel - Figure 8-6

File Edit View Insert Format Tools Data Window Help

C1 ▾ fx % of Coll Size

	A	B	C	D	E	F	G	H	I	J	K	L	M	N
1	Range	Items	% of Coll Size	Avg Pub	Med Pub	Total Circ	CY Circ	Items w/ Circ	% Items w/ Circ	Avg Circ	Items w/ Circ 05-06	Age / CY Use	Pub Last 5 Yrs	% of Recent Titles
2	000-099	3749	3	1992	1997	8887	1112	2269	61	2.4	743	-0.20	705	19
3	100-199	4524	4	1987	1990	11593	2144	3324	73	2.6	1334	-0.20	381	8
4	200-299	2400	2	1984	1988	5869	925	1659	69	2.4	630	-0.10	159	7
5	300-399	28414	25	1988	1991	52115	8367	16705	59	1.8	8367	-0.20	2548	9
6	400-499	3644	3	1986	1988	8962	1461	2317	64	2.5	849	-0.25	148	4
7	500-549	3919	3	1987	1990	16353	1752	2663	68	4.2	997	-0.19	241	6
8	550-599	3577	3	1984	1988	8926	1266	2497	70	2.5	826	-0.18	236	7
9	600-615	2887	2	1992	1995	9657	1661	2131	74	3.3	913	-0.23	461	16
10	615-625	5829	5	1991	1993	14673	2353	4002	69	2.5	1461	-0.23	760	13
11	626-650	4715	4	1989	1991	8768	1534	3094	66	1.9	1073	-0.24	606	13
12	651-699	4151	4	1991	1993	6895	1314	2370	57	1.6	123	-0.25	529	13
13	700-749	4157	4	1987	1990	15292	2633	3359	81	3.7	1491	-0.23	362	9
14	750-799	6813	6	1988	1991	30292	6672	5279	77	4.4	2680	-0.05	785	12
15	800-809	2636	2	1978	1983	3455	595	1227	47	1.3	363	-0.21	76	3
16	810-815	10093	9	1981	1986	14733	2257	5210	52	1.5	1583	-0.15	301	3
17	816-849	7320	6	1974	1977	8316	1262	3190	44	1.1	905	-0.15	123	2
18	850-899	3468	3	1980	1983	3958	562	1640	47	1.1	433	0.00	29	1
19	900-999	13496	12	1983	1988	27546	4370	8273	61	2.0	2808	-0.20	1069	8
20	TOTALS	115792	100			256290	42240	71209	61	2.2	27579		9519	8

Sheet1 / Sheet2 / Sheet3 /

Ready Count=20

We now see (in figure 8-6) that 000–099 is 3 percent of the collection, 300–399 is a whopping 25 percent, and so on. Now repeat the process of finding the percentage of circulation using the data in the Total Circ column. Insert a new column to the right of column C, and label it % of Tot Circ. The total circulation is 256,290. Divide the number of circulations for each Dewey range by that number, and multiply by 100 (=G2/256290*100). Click, hold, and drag, and format the cells for no decimal points.

Now we are ready to apply relative use. Insert one more column to the right of % of Tot Circ, label it Relative Use, and enter the formula to divide the percentage of circulation by the percentage of the collection size. In the example, that would be =D2/C2*100 (see figure 8-7). Click, hold, and drag for the column, and we now see relative use. Look at column E—Relative Use. Some very interesting things appear in the example. Remember, a relative use of 100 (or 1, if you didn't multiply the result by 100) means use for this part of the collection is balanced with the size of this part of the collection. For 000–099, the relative use is 107, meaning that these books are 7 percent more likely to be used than the collection as a whole. (If you are confused about why 3 divided by 3 times 100 isn't 100 in the example, that is because Excel figured in the hidden decimal numbers in columns C and D.)

The largest section, the 300s, has a relative use of only 83, meaning that items in this area receive 17 percent less use than the collection as a whole. In the 700s, books are used over twice the average! An area that we were worried about before, the two ranges of the 500s, now shows itself to be stronger than the collection as a whole. But in relative use and almost every other category, the 800s stink. Why is that? The age of the items is older, but then this is the literature section, where age isn't a big factor. Does it need weeding? Probably, but even if we look at the average circulation for those sections when only items that were used are counted,

FIGURE 8-7

Microsoft Excel - Figure 8-7

File   Edit   View   Insert   Format   Tools   Data   Window   Help

D1   fx   % of Total Circ

Range	Items	% of Coll Size	% of Total Circ	Relative Use	Total Circ	% of Recent Titles	Total Circ Items Pub Last 5 Yrs	Avg Circ New Items	#02-06 Pubs w/ Circ CY	YTD Circ for 02-06 Items	% New Items Used 2005-06
000-099	3749	3	3	107	8887	19	1910	2.7	295	523	42
100-199	4524	4	5	116	11593	8	931	2.4	225	456	59
200-299	2400	2	2	110	5869	7	411	2.6	82	143	52
300-399	28414	25	20	83	52115	9	5892	2.3	2283	2283	90
400-499	3644	3	3	111	8962	4	421	2.8	93	187	63
500-549	3919	3	6	189	16353	6	511	2.1	103	226	43
550-599	3577	3	3	113	8926	7	576	2.4	102	243	43
600-615	2887	2	4	151	9657	16	1792	3.9	255	657	55
615-625	5829	5	6	114	14673	13	1589	2.1	349	677	46
626-650	4715	4	3	84	8768	13	1013	1.7	300	504	50
651-699	4151	4	3	75	6895	13	1102	2.1	249	480	47
700-749	4157	4	6	166	15292	9	1045	2.9	209	550	58
750-799	6813	6	12	201	30292	12	3260	4.2	484	1652	62
800-809	2636	2	1	59	3455	3	189	2.5	39	95	51
810-815	10093	9	6	66	14733	3	802	2.7	138	328	46
816-849	7320	6	3	51	8316	2	326	2.7	56	125	46
850-899	3468	3	2	52	3958	1	42	1.4	13	15	45
900-999	13496	12	11	92	27546	8	2542	2.4	515	1071	48
TOTALS	115792	100	100	100	256290	8	24354	2.6	5790	10215	61

Sheet1 / Sheet2 / Sheet3

Ready   Count=40

the numbers are still low. The average use of new items in this part of the collection is close to that of the entire collection, but the percentage of new items used in the past year is about 20 percent less than the average. This means a few new items are receiving a lot of use, but many are not being used at all. Identify and buy more "hot" items and stop buying the cold ones. On a positive note, although the 300s have a low relative use, the percentage of new items used is 90 percent, the highest in the library (column U). Changes in buying seem to be turning this collection around.

We advise doing a collection use analysis yearly, or at longest, every two years. Then changes in age and use can be tracked over time. If the 800s are weeded and use rises, then you know you've solved some of the problem. If they are weeded and use remains low, it might be time to look at electronic use and buying practices. Another advantage of yearly analysis is that the library not only can track changes in use but can measure the rate of change in those changes as well.[3] For example, imagine a library that compared use of the quilting books with use of the history books and got these results:

	Year A Circ	Year B Circ	Increase in Circulation	Rate of Growth
Quilting	517	1,034	517	100%
History	5,000	5,517	517	10%

The increase in both cases is 517 uses, but the quilting section is experiencing faster growth than history. Rate of growth can also be applied to collection size.

Large Dewey or LC sections, although useful for explaining the process, are not the best way of looking at a collection. Use smaller ranges or, better, if your collection budget is tied to subjects that cover scattered classification numbers (and you have a good cheap worker to cut and paste them together), group the collection in that manner. There is no end to ways you can sort your collection's use.

There are also myriad ways of analyzing the data that are not presented here. If the collection budget is broken down by subject area, see how much each use in the current year (or last three years) cost.[4] If you have accurate book cost information in the item records, find out the average cost per item in the collection. We calculated relative use for total circulation since this library switched to its current ILS. Relative use should also be calculated using the most recent year's circulation. If you are looking for inspiration, two of the ideas that we found and liked in preparing this book follow.

Compare frequency of use per age of each document.[5] For example:

Pub Year	No. of Books	% of Collection	Use	% Use
1983	16	9	11	15

Lancaster and Sandore offer another way of checking collection use.[6] Find out what proportion of the library was borrowed in a staggered time frame. For example:

Level of Popularity	Measure	% of Collection
A	Borrowed last month	3
B	Borrowed last 3 months, but not last month	10
C	Borrowed last year, but not last 3 months	25
D	Borrowed last 5 years, but not last year	30
E	Not borrowed in last 5 years	32

Decide what analyses are best for your library, and do them. Save your raw data, so that you can go back and run old analyses to answer new questions.

You might have found the columns of numbers difficult to track and understand, or you might need to present this information to a manager, who may be pressed for time or afraid of numbers. The next chapter will help you solve that problem by showing you how Excel can highlight certain findings or present them in a graphical format.

NOTES

1. These numbers are consistent with the findings of the 1979 University of Pittsburgh study. In a six-year period, 40 percent of the items were never used, and, of items used

more than once, 73 percent of use occurred in the first two years after publication. Allen Kent et al., *Use of Library Materials: The University of Pittsburgh Study* (New York: Marcel Dekker, 1979), 9.

2. A. K. Jain et al., *Report on a Statistical Study of Book Use* (Lafayette, IN: Purdue University School of Industrial Engineering, 1967), 99, cited in Sharon Baker and F. Wilfrid Lancaster, *The Measurement and Evaluation of Library Services,* 2nd ed. (Arlington, VA: Information Resources Press, 1991).

3. M. Bavakutty and K. C. Abdul Majeed, *Methods of Measuring Quality of Libraries* (New Delhi: Ess Ess Publications, 2005), 149–50.

4. Karen Krueger, *Coordinated Cooperative Collection Development for Illinois Libraries* (Springfield: Illinois State Library, 1983), pt. 1, 20–21.

5. M. S. Sridhar, *Library Use and User Research: With 20 Case Studies* (New Delhi: Concept Publishing, 2002), 155–57.

6. F. W. Lancaster and Beth Sandore, *Technology and Management in Library and Information Services* (Champaign: University of Illinois Graduate School of Library and Information Science, 1997), 66.

Chapter 9

Presenting Your Findings with Color and Graphs

Now that you have your Excel worksheet populated with all the data that you need—how do you show it graphically to summarize your findings? Many times you may have all the right numbers to back up your decisions, but others may not have the time or desire to decipher it all. Using charts and highlighting information can help you present your findings to decision makers and colleagues in a concise manner.

Figure 9-1 is another copy of the *Summary* file we worked on in chapter 8, with the calculations completed. There is a lot of good data there, but how do you present it to people in a hurry, or to those intimidated by numbers? You can look at the file and see that in many categories, there are divisions of the collection that noticeably outperformed (or underperformed) the collection as a whole. How do you point those out? We are going to call those over and under divisions "variances," meaning they varied significantly from the norm. After we spot them, we are going to highlight them by putting a color background in those cells to draw the eye.

FIGURE 9-1

Microsoft Excel - Figure 9-1

File Edit View Insert Format Tools Data Window Help

A1   fx Range

	Range	Items	% of Coll Size	% of Total Circ	Relative Use	% of Items w/ Circ	Avg Circ	Correl Age / CY Use	% of Recent Titles	Avg Circ New Items	% New Items Used 2005-06
	A	B	C	D	E	K	L	N	P	R	U
2	000-099	3749	3	3	107	61	2.4	-0.20	19	2.7	42
3	100-199	4524	4	5	116	73	2.6	-0.20	8	2.4	59
4	200-299	2400	2	2	110	69	2.4	-0.10	7	2.6	52
5	300-399	28414	25	20	83	59	1.8	-0.20	9	2.3	90
6	400-499	3644	3	3	111	64	2.5	-0.25	4	2.8	63
7	500-549	3919	3	6	189	68	4.2	-0.19	6	2.1	43
8	550-599	3577	3	3	113	70	2.5	-0.18	7	2.4	43
9	600-615	2887	2	4	151	74	3.3	-0.23	16	3.9	55
10	615-625	5829	5	6	114	69	2.5	-0.23	13	2.1	46
11	626-650	4715	4	3	84	66	1.9	-0.24	13	1.7	50
12	651-699	4151	4	3	75	57	1.6	-0.25	13	2.1	47
13	700-749	4157	4	6	166	81	3.7	-0.23	9	2.9	58
14	750-799	6813	6	12	201	77	4.4	-0.05	12	4.2	62
15	800-809	2636	2	1	59	47	1.3	-0.21	3	2.5	51
16	810-815	10093	9	6	66	52	1.5	-0.15	3	2.7	46
17	816-849	7320	6	3	51	44	1.1	-0.15	2	2.7	46
18	850-899	3468	3	2	52	47	1.1	0.00	1	1.4	45
19	900-999	13496	12	11	92	61	2.0	-0.20	8	2.4	48
20	TOTALS	115792	100	100	100	61	2.2		8	2.6	61

Sheet1 / Sheet2 / Sheet3

Ready

Adding Color

In figure 9-1 we will concentrate on those columns that actually show analysis rather than raw numbers. Column E is Relative Use. The average for a collection is 100, so we decided to note any cells with relative uses more or less than 15 from that point. The cells that are 15 or more points above 100 are E3, 7, 9, 13, and 14. Those cells (which correspond to parts of the collection) show which parts of the collection circulated noticeably better than average. We will make them blue, in order to bring them out.

Right-click in cell E3, and choose **Format Cells.** Then click the tab that says **Patterns** (see figure 9-2). You have a range of colors to choose from. Click on a pretty blue, and click **OK.** (It will appear as light shading in this book's images.) Now you have a highlighted cell. You can repeat that process for the other cells that are in the "over" variance. Now, for the underachievers, looking at the same column, we see that E5, 11, 12, 15, 16, 17, and 18 all have 15 or more points *less* than 100. Mark these with a red or orange color to show a problem. (These will appear as darker shadings in this book's images.)

Figure 9-3 shows the result of this coloring, with several columns selected to highlight. Looking at the results across the rows, it is easy to see now that certain Dewey ranges generally outperformed the norm, as they have a number of blue cells going across. The same is true for the underperformers. The variances that were decided on for each column are typed below, so it is easy to know why certain cells were highlighted. Cells that are close to the norm were left alone.

Do the 800s ranges have low relative use because they have a low percentage of recent titles (column P)? Maybe yes, maybe no. Does the area need weeding? Are the students of this college using electronic resources for literary criticism instead

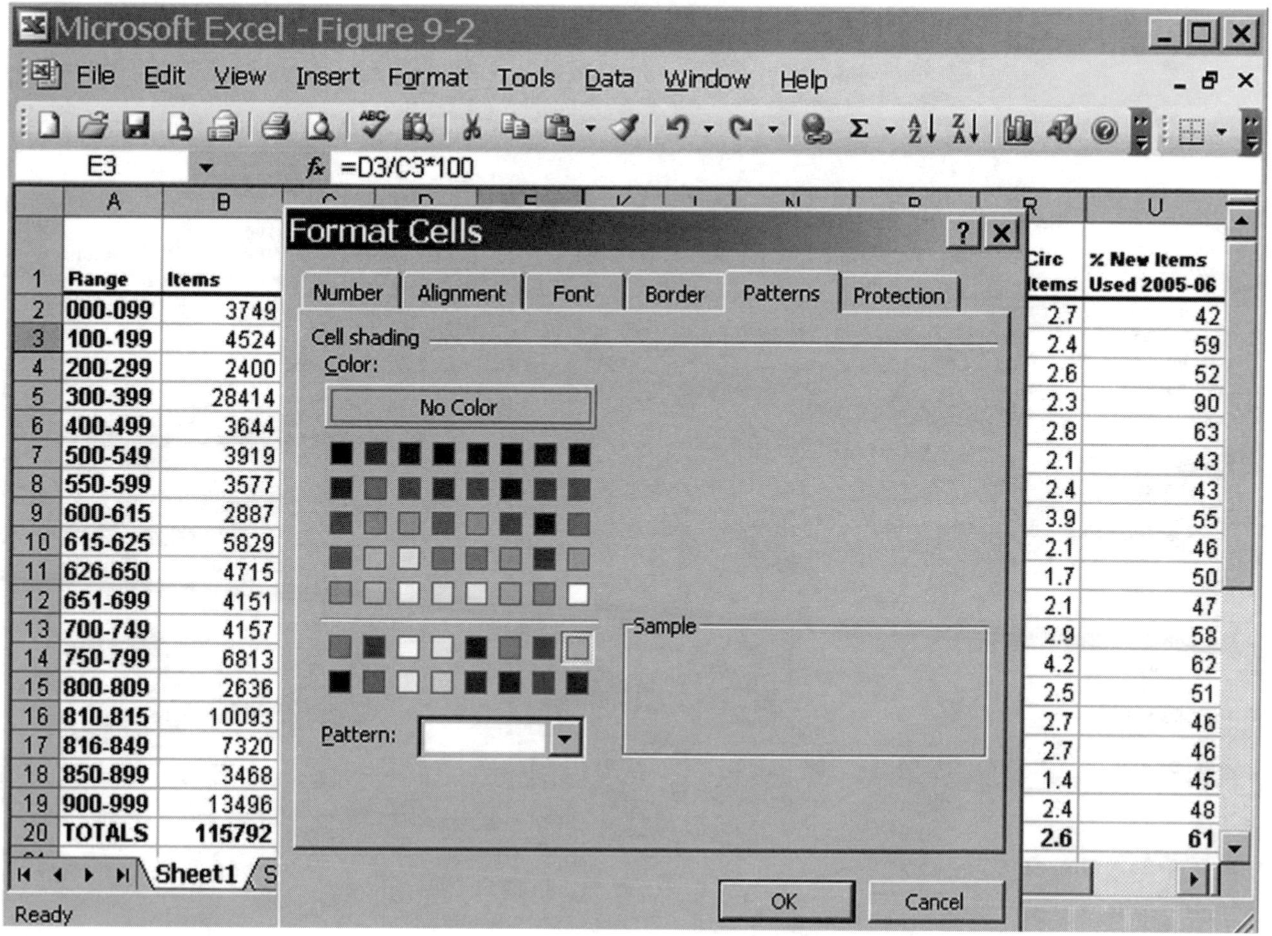

FIGURE 9-2

A screenshot of Microsoft Excel titled "Microsoft Excel - Figure 9-2" with the Format Cells dialog box open to the Patterns tab.

Cell reference: E3, formula bar: =D3/C3*100

	Range	Items
1	Range	Items
2	000-099	3749
3	100-199	4524
4	200-299	2400
5	300-399	28414
6	400-499	3644
7	500-549	3919
8	550-599	3577
9	600-615	2887
10	615-625	5829
11	626-650	4715
12	651-699	4151
13	700-749	4157
14	750-799	6813
15	800-809	2636
16	810-815	10093
17	816-849	7320
18	850-899	3468
19	900-999	13496
20	TOTALS	115792

Format Cells dialog — Tabs: Number, Alignment, Font, Border, Patterns, Protection

Cell shading
Color:
No Color
Pattern:
Sample

OK   Cancel

Circ Items	% New Items Used 2005-06
2.7	42
2.4	59
2.6	52
2.3	90
2.8	63
2.1	43
2.4	43
3.9	55
2.1	46
1.7	50
2.1	47
2.9	58
4.2	62
2.5	51
2.7	46
2.7	46
1.4	45
2.4	48
2.6	61

FIGURE 9-3

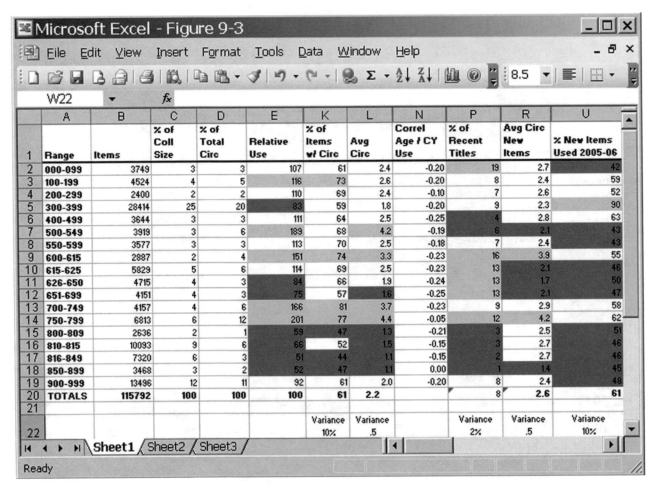

of books? Once again, you will have to use other information, and your experience and training, to make a decision. But now you know there is a problem in this area.

Making Graphs

As nice as the colored cells are, you might find that creating a graph is a better way to display some information. Excel can create graphs using the numerical information that you have in a spreadsheet. We will start with a simple graph (which Excel calls a chart), and then go to one that is more complex. We will start with a graph that will show the median age of the items in each collection range. Use the following steps:

Step 1. It is easier to make charts when the columns that you are comparing are lined up next to each other—so the first step in this case is to cut column G, Med Pub, select column B, and then choose **Insert–Cut Cells** from the Menu bar.

Step 2. Next, highlight the area that you want to compare—in this case A2 through B19 (see figure 9-4). (Don't highlight the totals and column headings.)

Step 3. Next, click on **Insert** and then **Chart**—this opens the Chart Wizard (figure 9-5).

Step 4. Choose the chart type that you desire—in this case choose **Column** and click **Next.**

Step 5. Now look in the lower left of the Chart Wizard (see figure 9-6). For the option Series in, select **Columns** and click **Next.**

FIGURE 9-4

Microsoft Excel - Figure 9-4

File   Edit   View   Insert   Format   Tools   Data   Window   Help

A2   fx 000-099

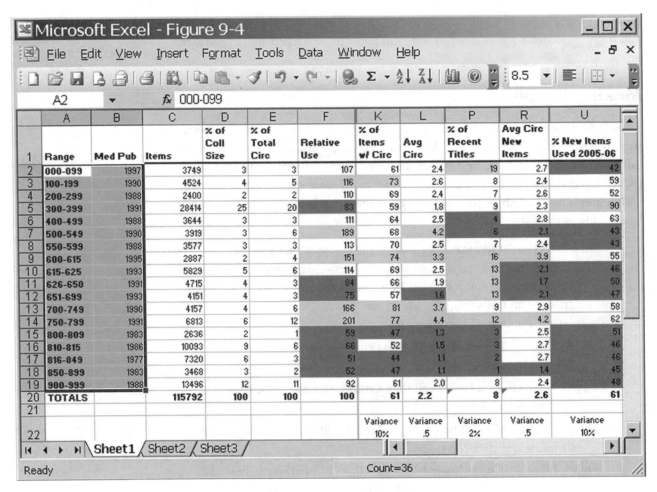

Range	Med Pub	Items	% of Coll Size	% of Total Circ	Relative Use	% of Items w/ Circ	Avg Circ	% of Recent Titles	Avg Circ New Items	% New Items Used 2005-06
000-099	1997	3749	3	3	107	61	2.4	19	2.7	42
100-199	1990	4524	4	5	116	73	2.6	8	2.4	59
200-299	1988	2400	2	2	110	69	2.4	7	2.6	52
300-399	1991	28414	25	20	83	59	1.8	9	2.3	90
400-499	1988	3644	3	3	111	64	2.5	4	2.8	63
500-549	1990	3919	3	6	189	68	4.2	6	2.1	43
550-599	1988	3577	3	3	113	70	2.5	7	2.4	43
600-615	1995	2887	2	4	151	74	3.3	16	3.9	55
615-625	1993	5829	5	6	114	69	2.5	13	2.1	46
626-650	1991	4715	4	3	84	66	1.9	13	1.7	50
651-699	1993	4151	4	3	75	57	1.6	13	2.1	47
700-749	1990	4157	4	6	166	81	3.7	9	2.9	58
750-799	1991	6813	6	12	201	77	4.4	12	4.2	62
800-809	1983	2636	2	1	59	47	1.3	3	2.5	51
810-815	1986	10093	9	6	66	52	1.5	3	2.7	46
816-849	1977	7320	6	3	51	44	1.1	2	2.7	46
850-899	1983	3468	3	2	52	47	1.1	1	1.4	45
900-999	1988	13496	12	11	92	61	2.0	8	2.4	48
TOTALS		115792	100	100	100	61	2.2	8	2.6	61
						Variance 10%	Variance .5	Variance 2%	Variance .5	Variance 10%

Sheet1 / Sheet2 / Sheet3

Ready   Count=36

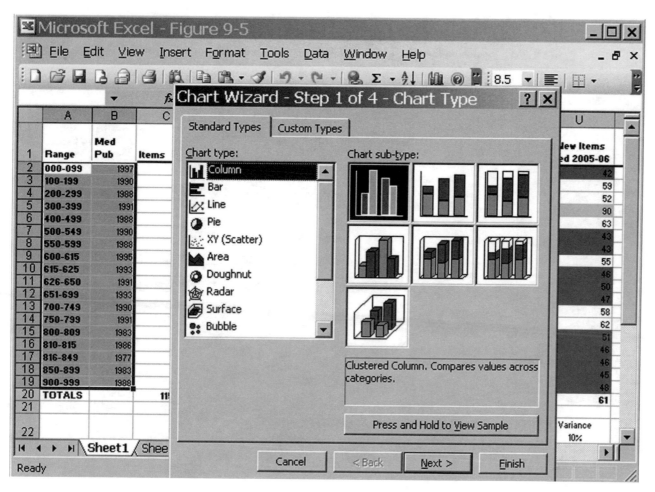

FIGURE 9-5

FIGURE 9-6

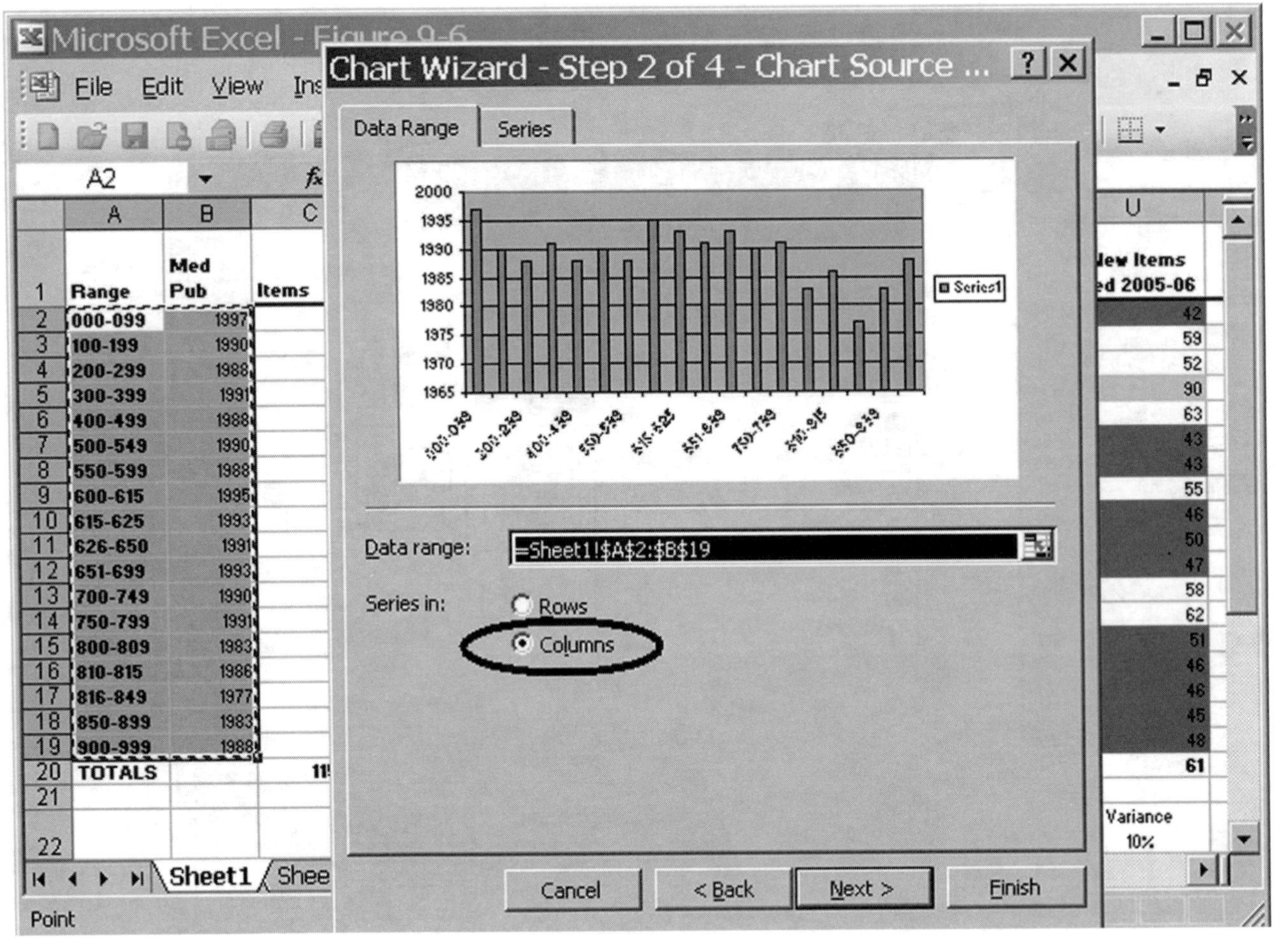
Microsoft Excel - Figure 9-6
File Edit View Ins
Chart Wizard - Step 2 of 4 - Chart Source ...
Data Range
Series
A2
Range
Med Pub
Items
000-099 1997
100-199 1990
200-299 1988
300-399 1991
400-499 1988
500-549 1990
550-599 1988
600-615 1995
615-625 1993
626-650 1991
651-699 1993
700-749 1990
750-799 1991
800-809 1983
810-815 1986
816-849 1977
850-899 1983
900-999 1988
TOTALS
Series1
Data range:
=Sheet1!$A$2:$B$19
Series in:
Rows
Columns
Cancel
< Back
Next >
Finish
Sheet1
Point
Variance
10%

Step 6. Now look at figure 9-7. It is time to give your chart a title and to label the x-axis (across) and the y-axis (up). Title this chart Median Pub Date by Collection Range. Label the x-axis Collection Range and the y-axis Median Pub Date and click **Next.**

Step 7. Your last choice is to display the chart as a new sheet or as an object in the sheet (see figure 9-8). In this case, choose **As new sheet** and click **Finish.** (If you selected **As object in,** Excel would place the chart inside an existing sheet. Creating a new sheet is easier to handle.)

Step 8. Now Excel creates a new tab in the workbook (or file) that had our original data and calls it Chart 1 (see figure 9-9).

Step 9. The chart will appear as a separate worksheet in your workbook. Remember, you can change the name with a right-click on the tab.

FIGURE 9-7

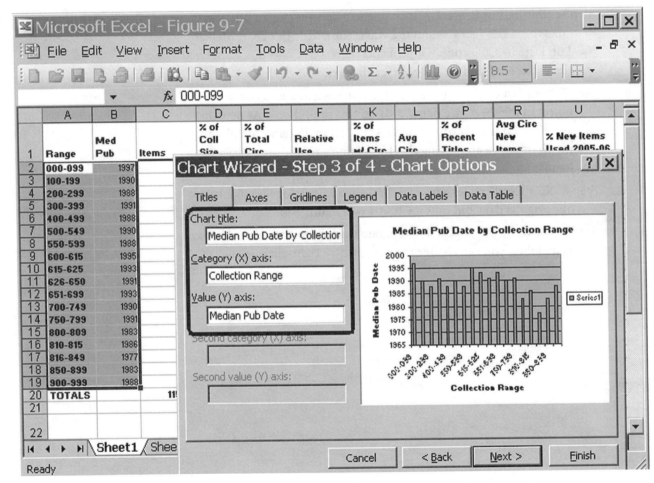

FIGURE 9-8

FIGURE 9-8

Range	Med Pub	Items	% of Coll Size	% of Total Circ	Relative Use	% of Items w/ Circ	Avg Circ	% of Recent Titles	Avg Circ New Items	% New Items Used 2005-06
000-099	1997	3749	3	3	107	61	2.4	19	2.7	42
100-199	1990	4524	4	5	116	73	2.6	8	2.4	59
200-299	1988	2400	2	2	110	69	2.4	7	2.6	52
300-399	1991	28414	25	20	83	59	1.8	9	2.3	90
400-499	1988	3644	3	3	111	64	2.5	4	2.8	63
500-549	1990	3919	3	6	189	68	4.2	6	2.1	43
550-599	1988	3577	3	3	113	70	2.5	7	2.4	43
600-615	1995	2887	2	4	151	74	3.3	16	3.9	55
615-625	1993	5829	5	6	114	69	2.5	13	2.1	46
626-650	1991	4715	4	3	84	66	1.9	13	1.7	50
651-699	1993									47
700-749	1990									58
750-799	1991									62
800-809	1983									51
810-815	1986									46
816-849	1977									46
850-899	1983									45
900-999	1988									48
TOTALS		11!								61

Chart Wizard - Step 4 of 4 - Chart Location

Place chart:

○ As new sheet: Chart1

○ As object in: Sheet1

Cancel   < Back   Next >   Finish

FIGURE 9-9

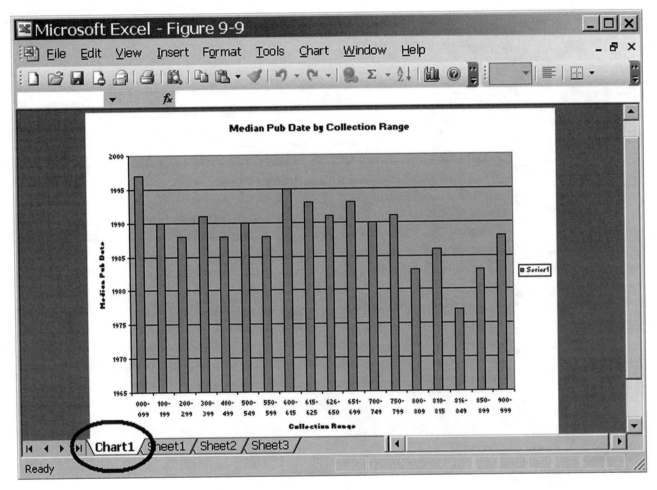

Graphs Comparing Two Different Sets of Data

Now it is time to make a more complex chart. In this case, for each Dewey range in our *Summary* file, we will compare the percentage of collection size to the percentage of circulation. There are three sets of information: Dewey range, percentage of collection, and percentage of circulation.

Step 1. As before, it is easier to make charts when the columns that you are comparing are lined up next to each other. So, going back to the *Summary* file, the first step in this case is to cut columns D and E, the circulation and collection percentages, and then insert the cut cells next to column A, which has the Dewey ranges. (Don't paste—you have to use **Insert–Cut Cells** to maintain the file's integrity.) Now again highlight the numbers in those three columns, as in figure 9-10. (Again, just the regular numbers are highlighted—the totals and the column headings are not included.)

Step 2. Next, click on **Insert** and then **Chart**—this opens the Chart Wizard, which you used for the first chart.

Step 3. Choose the chart type that you desire—again choose **Column** (see figure 9-10). Now look at the little images of different chart sub-types. Select the one that shows one column standing behind another, Chart sub-type 3-D Column. (If you do a single click on each image, you will get a little description of what the chart does. In this case, the chart "Compares values across categories.") Now click **Next.**

FIGURE 9-10

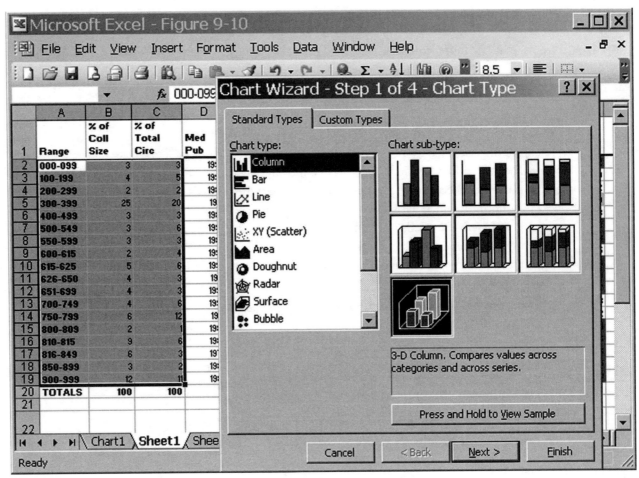

Step 4. Now look at figure 9-11. As before, select **Columns.** Then, on the same screen, click on the **Series** tab and enter % Coll (for "percentage of collection") in the Name box and then select **Series2** in the Series box. Notice that the Name box is again blank. This is because you are now going to name the second series, so click in the Name box again and this time type % Circ. Then click **Next.**

Step 5. Now it is time to title the chart and label the x-axis and z-axis. In this case, title the chart % Collection versus % Circulation. Then label the x-axis (that is the across one) Range (for Dewey range) and leave the y-axis blank. Notice that there is another axis for this chart (because it is 3-D). Label this z-axis Percentage. Still on step 3 of the wizard, click on the **Axes** tab and *deselect* the Series (y) axis. Then click **Next.**

Step 6. Your last choice is to display the chart as a new sheet or as an object in an existing sheet. Choose **As new sheet,** call it Chart 2, and click **Finish.**

Step 7. The chart will appear as separate worksheet (those tabs on the bottom) in your workbook and should look like figure 9-12.

You might wonder why we had you avoid the y-axis for this 3-D chart. In this case, we didn't need to label it, so we left it out to provide more space. You can certainly experiment with it and see how things look. In fact, you should experiment with different types of charts. You will find that for different types and amounts of data, different charts work better than others.

Well, you did it. You crunched numbers, you compiled them into a *Summary* file, and you learned some presentation tricks. As you have figured out by now,

FIGURE 9-11

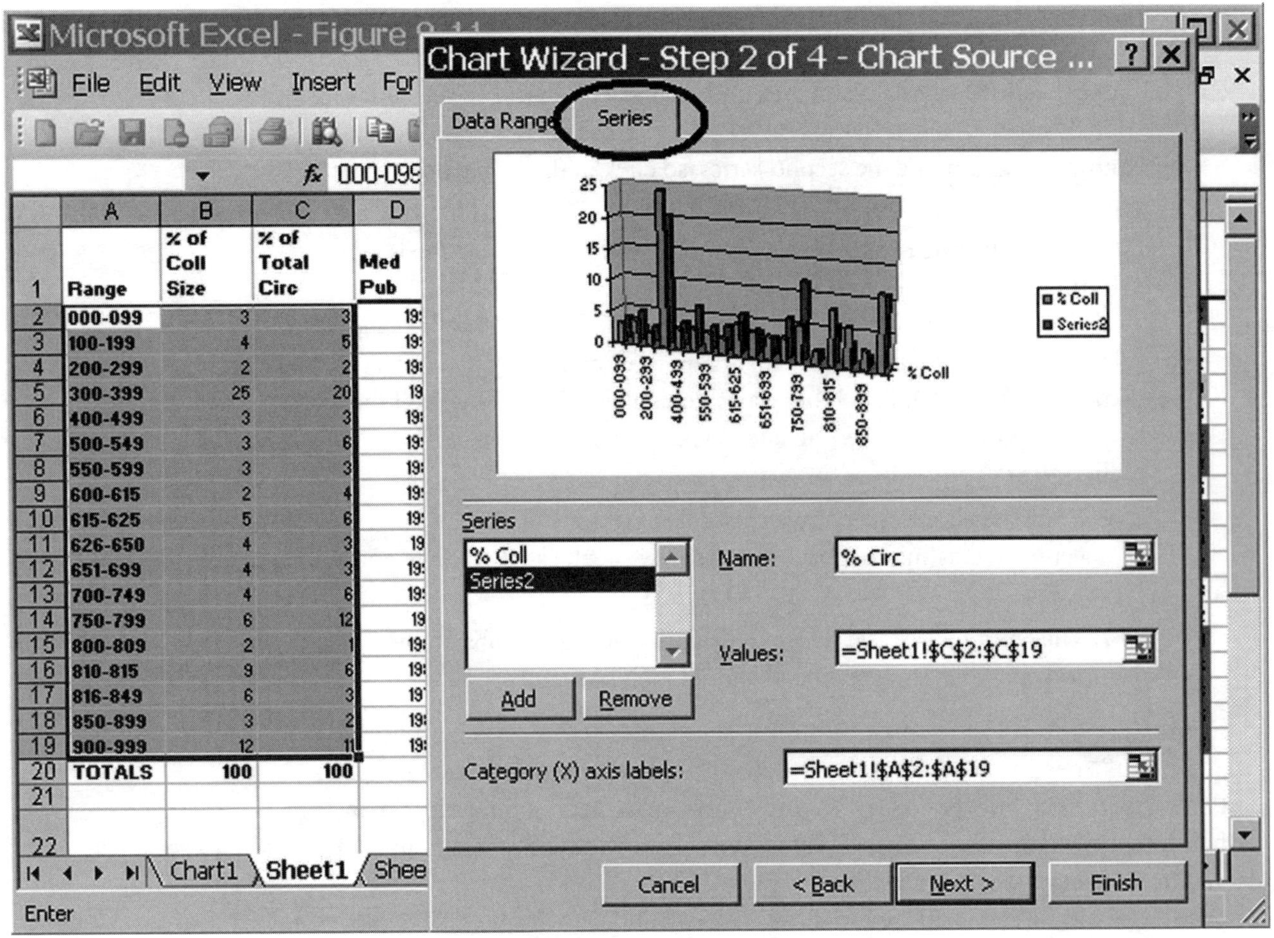

Microsoft Excel - Figure 9-11
Chart Wizard - Step 2 of 4 - Chart Source ...
File Edit View Insert For
Data Range
Series
000-099
Range
% of Coll Size
% of Total Circ
Med Pub
000-099 3 3
100-199 4 5
200-299 2 2
300-399 25 20
400-499 3 3
500-549 3 6
550-599 3 3
600-615 2 4
615-625 5 6
626-650 4 3
651-699 4 3
700-749 4 6
750-799 6 12
800-809 2 1
810-815 9 6
816-849 6 3
850-899 3 2
900-999 12 11
TOTALS 100 100
% Coll
Series2
Name: % Circ
Values: =Sheet1!$C$2:$C$19
Add
Remove
Category (X) axis labels: =Sheet1!$A$2:$A$19
Cancel
< Back
Next >
Finish
Chart1
Sheet1
Enter

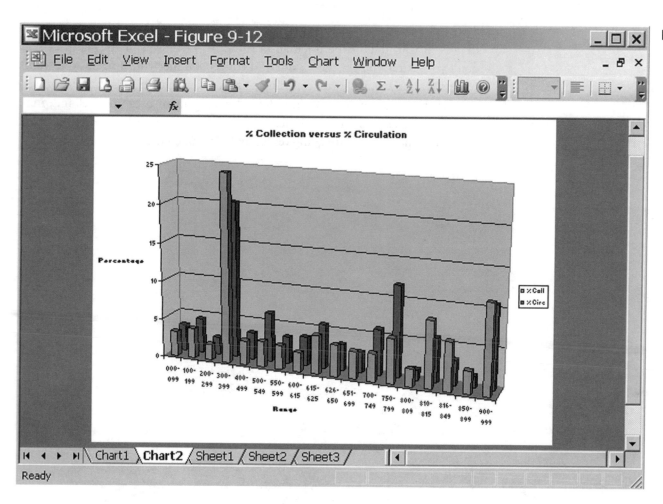

FIGURE 9-12

there is no end to the ways you can compare numbers and quite a variety of ways to present your data. Experimentation is the key—you've still got that *Clean* file, don't you? After you get these skills and concepts under your fingers, you will be surprised at how quickly you can run an analysis and create a graph. After you are comfortable, read chapter 10 on potential management uses of Excel and, more important, areas where research needs to be done and published. Good luck, and let us know how things are going (excelbook@gmail.com).

Management Uses of Excel and Future Research

There are many possible ways of using Excel to measure use of the library without being specifically limited to the collection. Not all require calculations. For those that do, the procedures to follow should now be clear. As with the various ways to analyze collection use, it is doubtful that any library will find all of these useful. Pick the ones that interest you, ignore the rest, and happy crunching. Increased value will come in having these numbers to compare year after year after year.

Management Statistics to Consider Compiling

1. Items in the collection (and subcategories of the collection: nonfiction, children's, YA, videos, DVDs, etc.).
2. Items added to the collection and its sections, over a set period, usually a year. (Download your collection data, with a "catalog date" field.)
3. Items chosen by each selector (collection development librarian or faculty, depending on the institution).[1]
4. Circulation (or combined circulation and in-house use) divided by library budget, and the library's collection budget. (In other words, what did a use cost, in terms of the collection budget and the library's budget as a whole?)

5. Circulation per registered user. (Although public libraries will look at average circulation per community member, academic libraries may follow George Jenks's idea of comparing circulation in a subject area to enrollment in that same area.)[2]
6. Circulation per population in the service area.
7. Circulation per hours of operation, and for each specific hour of operation.
8. Circulation per day of the week.
9. Circulation per volume (or item) in the collection.
10. Circulation per title. (Multiple copies of one title would have their use combined.)
11. Circulation per FTE.
12. Circulation per shelf or shelf range.[3]
13. Circulation per FTE professional staff.
14. Titles owned. (Download the data by bibliographic record, not item.)
15. Circulation per square foot.
16. Circulation of periodicals per periodical (either volumes or titles).
17. Circulation per staff salary. (How much in staff salary did a circulation cost?)
18. Circulation per computer, broken down by staff, OPAC, and general-access computers.
19. Number of items (and the percentage of the collection) used in a set period, usually a year.
20. Door count per hour/location.
21. What percentage of library card holders used their card over the last year? Is there a relationship between the length of holding a card and the patron's sex, age, or ZIP code (which can be tied to a census tract)?[4]

22. For academic libraries: circulation in a subject area divided by student FTE in that area.[5]
23. For academic libraries: what percentage of students ever borrow a book? What is circulation per student for those who do borrow?[6]

Cost per Use and per Item

Cost per use is fairly simple to determine, if we leave long-term storage costs out of the equation. If a library has retained accurate price information for its items, those numbers can be totaled and divided by use to determine cost per use. This will work best with items added in the last year or two, and their own circulation. Average cost per item can be calculated by adding the cost of items purchased over the last year or two and dividing by the number of items. We include these calculations in the management chapter because they can be controversial and lead to bad feelings among staff members. We think they are an important analysis to have in hand when budgeting, but handle these numbers with care.

Geoffrey Ford's study of the relationship of budgeting to use in academic libraries found that almost 60 percent of the "document exposure" provided by academic libraries can be tied to expenditure per student.[7] The direct relationship between expenditure and use is true for colleges with enrollments up to 18,000.[8]

At the staff level, use studies can unintentionally lead to staff member embarrassment. The librarian with collection development responsibilities in an underused area may feel that her or his skills as a selector are being challenged. The approach to take is to address the librarian's personal skills: "Wow, we've learned from this study that patrons aren't using books in your investing area. You've got a good knowledge of that collection—take a look at your collection and this use study, and see what changes we need to make." Then be sure to praise the librarian when use begins to rise.

Comparative Data for Public Libraries

It seems that public libraries are more likely than academic ones to use comparative statistics to improve their service. We caution against comparing use of one library with that of another, believing there are too many variables to make one-to-one comparisons useful. However, there may be value in comparing your library's use figures to those for many other libraries. For public libraries, Bob Molyneux has set up a website called the Normative Data Project for Libraries (http://www .libraryndp.info/index.html) in which you can place use figures for your library and see how they compare to those of other public libraries. There is a fee involved for some of the information.

The Hennen Surveys are a very interesting attempt to develop consistent ratings of libraries, based on a lot of factors, including per-capita use, staff levels, and a variety of other measures. Thomas Hennen has tweaked his formula over the years in response to criticism and suggestions, and his ratings system is gaining acceptance. Certainly highly ranked libraries now trumpet that rating, even as lower-ranked libraries grumble that the system is unfair. We think Mr. Hennen is driving libraries to look at what they do and how they do it, and that can only improve things. The lists of "best" libraries by size are published annually in *American Libraries.* More can be found at http://www.haplr-index.com.

The Public Library Association, a division of the American Library Association, puts out an annual and extensive collection of public library statistics, called the

Public Library Data Statistical Report. It is aimed at "big picture" statistics and identifies library resources, annual use (for the library as a whole), and use of technology. At this point, it is most suitable for larger libraries.

Electronic Books

The problems of applying this analysis method to electronic books are discussed in chapter 5. Different vendors have different methods of counting use. Is a use a viewing, a search, or a download? The folks at NISO, the National Information Standards Organization, are addressing this problem with SUSHI—the Standardized Usage Statistics Harvesting Initiative. The idea is to have consistent use information from electronic database vendors. SUSHI (in beta at this writing) aims to standardize practice. More can be found at http://www.niso.org/committees/SUSHI/SUSHI_story.html.

An interesting study in 2005 compared use patterns of books that were available in both electronic and print format at the Louisiana State University Library. It found that the different formats had different use patterns, even for the same title.[9] More of this type of work is being done, and although electronic books as a whole remain a little-used and generally disliked part of library collections, there are niche areas in which they do well. Google and other companies are betting that the day will come when electronic books will be popular. Perhaps they are right. If you want to explore this further, we recommend the following:

> Bertot, John Carlo, and Denise M. Davis. *Planning and Evaluating Networked Services and Resources.* Libraries Unlimited, 2004.

Bertot, John Carlo, et al. "Capture Usage with E-Metrics." *Library Journal* 129, no. 8 (May 2004).

Bertot, John Carlo, et al. *Developing a National Data Collection Model for Public Library Network Statistics and Performance Measures: A Final Report.* Institute of Museum and Library Services, 2002. http://www.ii.fsu.edu.

Bertot, John Carlo, et al. *Statistics and Performance Measures for Public Library Network Statistics.* American Library Association, 2001.

Christianson, Marilyn, and Marsha Aucoin. "Electronic or Print Books: Which Are Used?" *Library Collections, Acquisitions and Technical Services* 29 (2005): 71–81.

Shim, Wonsik, et al. *Data Collection Manual for Academic and Research Library Network Statistics and Performance Measures.* Association of Research Libraries, 2001.

Areas for Future Research

One of the weaknesses in the library profession is the lack of core texts and research upon which our profession rests. An ironic reason for this may be the low quality of our periodical indexes. It is difficult and frustrating to find relevant material about a topic when the subject term "collection development" includes use studies, collection-centered analysis methods such as Conspectus, buying suggestions, "how I did it" articles, and a plethora of other topics. To complicate matters, our profession has not used consistent terminology over the years. Our research found relevant articles using phrases like "Operations Research," "Informetrics," and

"Use Studies." (There are also things called "User studies" but they are about what one individual does with library material.)

In collection analysis, we think the work of F. W. Lancaster, A. K. Jain, and the University of Pittsburgh study are seminal works, but many librarians may not know of them. Others doubtlessly have favorite studies of their own. The point is that librarians do not have a common frame of reference for professional research and discussion. Even worse, what is often "known" from these works is often wrong. For example, references are often made to the "80-20" rule, which is the idea that 20 percent of the collection accounts for 80 percent of the use. Although studies have consistently shown that a comparatively small number of items accounts for most of the use, the 80-20 rule is hardly universal. The University of Pittsburgh study, for example, showed that 80 percent of the use in that library came from 42 percent of the collection.[10]

Stanley Slote showed that weeding books with little or no use from a collection will increase circulation. For too many librarians, it has become a truism that weeding on any criteria will increase circulation. The profession, in particular library schools, needs to step up to the plate and get this in order.

Our goal here is to suggest a few areas in which research needs to be done or classic studies need to be updated. For example, we could really use reports on how collections are used at various libraries. What percentage of your library's collection accounts for 80 percent of use? Find out, send it in to some library publication, and tell us! If this is done frequently from a number of institutions, researchers will have a data pool larger than a study at one library from which to develop formulas and theories of library use that may actually be universal.

A. K. Jain's study showed that material age was not a particular deterrent to use for some parts of Purdue University's collection. However, his study was done in the card catalog days. Contemporary catalogs typically present search results in a chronological fashion. Do patrons only seek the items they find on the first screen? Do they still browse once they find a relevant call number? Is Jain's finding still true? Run a correlation on your data, and tell us!

Areas of Collection Analysis That Need Study or Updating

- Does "filling holes" in a collection by purchasing recommended titles from a bibliography improve circulation?
- How many days is the typical circulation period for public library fiction? Nonfiction? Children's books? (This can lead to better systems of buying multiple copies of popular books.)
- Sharon Baker and F. W. Lancaster, in *The Measurement and Evaluation of Library Services* (1991), mention several studies (see page 82) that showed that collection use changed slowly over time. However, these are pre-Internet studies. Is this still true?
- Is there a correlation of age to use for certain material types (do videos "get old" before books)?
- Some computer systems allow a compiled "log" of all patron search attempts. These are sometimes studied in an effort to better design OPACs. They could also be studied to see if the library had in its collection (1) known title items searched by patrons (i.e., title searches), (2) authors searched by patrons, and, more ambitiously, (3) satisfactory results from keyword searches.
- What is the correlation of amount spent in an area to use in that area?

- Between different libraries with similar demographics, what is the correlation of staff salary to use? Of staff salary to door count? Of library budget to door count or use?
- How does use of items purchased on standing order plans compare to use of items selected by staff? (Probably best for nonfiction.)
- Altmann and Gorman's 1999 study of academic libraries in Australia showed that journal impact factors were poor indicators of local use. Is this true in other libraries?[11]
- A 1989 study of academic libraries showed that students in various disciplines are "exposed" to documents at different rates. Over half of those differences were accounted for by library expenditure per student. In other words, the more money spent in a collection area, the more likely students were to use that area.[12] Now that web-based periodical collections are common and fairly easy to use, is this still true?
- The University of Pittsburgh study of 1979 showed that 79 percent of the titles that circulated also had internal use.[13] This argues against the bother of counting internal use. But that study is over twenty-five years old. Is there still a strong relationship between circulation and internal use?
- Another study, by Aguilar, found that interlibrary loan use was strongly related to use of the borrowing libraries' own collections.[14] That is, heavy local use of an area in a library meant heavy ILL borrowing, and low local use in an area corresponded to low ILL borrowing. However, that study was made in 1986, before shared cooperative catalogs became commonplace. Is this still true?

- Holds are a major concern of public libraries. Modern ILSs keep track of the number of holds on a title at a given point of time, but we don't know of any study that shows how many holds were placed but either canceled or never picked up.
- The holy grail of public library collections is the answer to this question: How many copies of a popular book should be purchased to meet user demand, as expressed by holds? If we can find the average number of days that a book with waiting holds is checked out, and how many holds are canceled or not picked up, then public libraries would be closer to finding a purchasing formula that would best use their resources.

You, dear reader, should pick one of these, study it, and write it up.

NOTES

1. F. W. Lancaster and Beth Sandore, *Technology and Management in Library and Information Services* (Champaign: University of Illinois Graduate School of Library and Information Science, 1997), 72.
2. George M. Jenks, "Circulation and Its Relationship to the Book Collection and Academic Departments," *College and Research Libraries* 37, no. 2 (March 1976): 93.
3. Tony Greiner, "Collection Development and Shelf Space: A Proposal for Nonfiction Collections," *Public Libraries* (November/December 2005): 43–46.
4. K. E. Dowlin and L. Magrath, "Beyond the Numbers: A Decision Support System," in *Library Automation as a Source of Management Information*, ed. F. W. Lancaster (Champaign: University of Illinois Graduate School of Library and Information Science, 1983), 30.
5. Jenks, "Circulation and Its Relationship," 145–52.

6. P. Barkley, "Patterns of Student Use of a College Library," *College and Research Libraries* 57 (February 1966): 103–6, found that about 62 percent of students did not borrow a book over two terms and 15 percent borrowed four or more. Barkley also found evidence that students who borrowed books at a higher rate had a higher grade point average. Cited in Aridaman K. Jain, "A Statistical Study of Book Use" (PhD thesis, Purdue University, 1967), 174–75.

7. Geoffrey Ford, "A Perspective on Performance Measurement," *International Journal of Information and Library Research* 1, no. 1 (1989): 21, cited in C. D. Emery, "The Acquisitions Budget and Student Borrowing Trends: An Examination of Some Evidence for a Statistical Relationship," in *Conference on Acquisitions, Budgets, and Collections, St. Louis Missouri, May 16 and 17, 1990: Proceedings,* ed. David C. Genaway (Canfield, OH: Genaway, 1990).

8. Emery, "The Acquisitions Budget," 100, 112–13.

9. Marilyn Christianson and Marsha Aucoin, "Electronic or Print Books: Which Are Used?" *Library Collections, Acquisitions and Technical Services* 29 (2005): 71–81.

10. Allen Kent et al., *Use of Library Materials: The University of Pittsburgh Study* (New York: Marcel Dekker, 1979), 38.

11. Klaus G. Altmann and G. E. Gorman, "The Usefulness of Impact Factors in Serial Selection: A Rank and Mean Analysis Using Ecology Journals," *Library Acquisitions* 22, no. 2 (1998): 147–59.

12. Ford, "A Perspective on Performance Measurement," 21.

13. Kent et al., *Use of Library Materials,* 26.

14. W. Aguilar, "The Application of Relative Use and Interlibrary Demand in Collection Development," *Collection Management* 8, no. 1 (1986): 15–24, cited in Lancaster and Sandore, *Technology and Management,* 72.

Bibliography

Aguilar, W. "The Application of Relative Use and Interlibrary Demand in Collection Development." *Collection Management* 8, no. 1 (1986): 15–24.

Altmann, Klaus G., and G. E. Gorman. "The Usefulness of Impact Factors in Serial Selection: A Rank and Mean Analysis Using Ecology Journals." *Library Acquisitions* 22, no. 2 (1998): 147–59.

Baker, Sharon, and F. Wilfrid Lancaster. *The Measurement and Evaluation of Library Services,* 2nd ed. Arlington, VA: Information Resources Press, 1991.

Barkely, P. "Patterns of Student Use of a College Library." *College and Research Libraries* 57 (February 1966): 103–6.

Bavakutty, M., and K. C. Abdul Majeed. *Methods of Measuring Quality of Libraries.* New Delhi: Ess Ess Publications, 2005.

Bertot, John Carlo, and Denise M. Davis. *Planning and Evaluating Networked Services and Resources.* Libraries Unlimited, 2004.

Bertot, John Carlo, et al. "Capture Usage with E-Metrics." *Library Journal* 129, no. 8 (May 2004).

Bertot, John Carlo, et al. *Developing a National Data Collection Model for Public Library Network Statistics and Performance Measures: A Final Report.* Institute of Museum and Library Services, 2002. http://www.ii.fsu.edu/projectFiles/collection-models/natl.model.final.report.pdf.

Bertot, John Carlo, et al. *Statistics and Performance Measures for Public Library Network Statistics.* American Library Association, 2001.

Brooks, Terrence A. "Naïve vs. Sophisticated Methods of Forecasting Public Library Circulation." *Library and Information Science Research* 6, no. 2 (April–June 1984): 205–14.

Buckland, Michael K. *Book Availability and the Library User.* New York: Pergamon Press, 1975.

Buczinski, James Andrew. "Debunking the Computer Science Digital Library: Lessons Learned in Collection Development at Seneca College of Applied Arts and Technology." *Acquisitions Librarian* 18, no. 35/36 (2006): 37–53.

Carrigan, D. P. "Data-Guided Collection Development: A Promise Unfulfilled." *College and Research Libraries* 57 (1996): 429–37.

Christianson, Marilyn, and Marsha Aucoin. "Electronic or Print Books: Which Are Used?" *Library Collections, Acquisitions, and Technical Services* 29 (2005): 71–81.

Day, Mike, and Don Revill. "Towards the Active Collection: The Use of Circulation Analysis in Collection Evaluation." *Journal of Librarianship and Information Science* 27, no. 3 (1995): 149–57.

D'Elia, George, et al. "Impact of the Internet on Public Library Use." *Journal of the American Society for Information Science* 53, no. 10 (2002): 802–20.

Doll, Carol A., and Pamela Petrick Barron. *Managing and Analyzing Your Collection: A Practical Guide for Small Libraries and School Media Centers.* Chicago: American Library Association, 2002.

Dowlin, K. E., and L. Magrath. "Beyond the Numbers: A Decision Support System." In *Library Automation as a Source of Management Information,* edited by F. W. Lancaster, 27–58. Champaign: University of Illinois Graduate School of Library and Information Science, 1983.

Emery, C. D. "The Acquisitions Budget and Student Borrowing Trends: An Examination of Some Evidence for a Statistical Relationship." In *Conference on Acquisitions, Budgets, and Collections, St. Louis Missouri, May 16 and 17, 1990: Proceedings,* ed. David C. Genaway. Canfield, OH: Genaway, 1990.

Faigel, Martin. "Methods and Issues in Collection Evaluation Today." *Library Acquisitions: Practice and Theory* 9 (1985): 21–35.

Ford, Geoffrey. "A Perspective on Performance Measurement." *International Journal of Information and Library Research* 1, no. 1 (1989): 12–23.

Fussler, Herman H., and Julian L. Simon. *Patterns of Use of Books in Large Research Libraries.* Chicago: University of Chicago Press, 1969.

Gabriel, Michael. *Collection Development and Collection Evaluation: A Sourcebook.* Metuchen, NJ: Scarecrow, 1995.

Genaway, David C., ed. *Conference on Acquisitions, Budgets, and Collections, St. Louis Missouri, May 16 and 17, 1990: Proceedings.* Canfield, OH: Genaway, 1990.

Greiner, Tony. "Collection Development and Shelf Space: A Proposal for Nonfiction Collections." *Public Libraries* (November/December 2005): 43–46.

Hamburg, Morris, Leonard Ramist, and Michael Bommer. "Library Objectives and Performance Measures and Their Use in Decision Making." *Library Quarterly* 42, no. 1 (January 1972): 107–28.

Jain, A. K., et al. *Report on a Statistical Study of Book Use.* Lafayette, IN: Purdue University School of Industrial Engineering, 1967.

Jain, Aridaman K. "A Statistical Study of Book Use." PhD Thesis, Purdue University, 1967.

Jenks, George M. "Circulation and Its Relationship to the Book Collection and Academic Departments." *College and Research Libraries* 37, no. 2 (March 1976): 145–52.

Kent, Allen, et al. *Use of Library Materials: The University of Pittsburgh Study.* New York: Marcel Dekker, 1979.

Knievel, Jennifer E., Heather Wicht, and Lynn S. Connaway. "Use of Circulation Statistics and Interlibrary Loan Data in Collection Management." *College and Research Libraries* (January 2006): 35–49.

Krueger, Karen. *Coordinated Cooperative Collection Development for Illinois Libraries.* Springfield: Illinois State Library, 1983.

Lancaster, F. W., and Beth Sandore. *Technology and Management in Library and Information Services.* Champaign: University of Illinois Graduate School of Library and Information Science, 1997.

Levine, Marilyn. "The Circulation/Acquisition Ratio: An Input-Output Measure for Libraries." *Information Processing and Management* 16, no. 6 (June 1980): 313–15.

Magrill, Rose Mary, and Doralyn J. Hickey. *Acquisitions Management and Collection Development in Libraries.* Chicago: American Library Association, 1984.

Moon, E. E. "Dewey Proportions." *Library Journal* 91 (June 1, 1966): 2783.

Ranck, S. H. "The Problem of the Unused Book." *Library Journal* 36 (1911): 428–29.

Rochell, Carlton. *Wheeler and Goldhor's Practical Administration of Public Libraries.* Rev. ed. New York: Harper and Row, 1980.

Shim, Wonsik, et al. *Data Collection Manual for Academic and Research Library Network Statistics and Performance Measures.* Association of Research Libraries, 2001.

Sridhar, M. S. *Library Use and User Research: With 20 Case Studies.* New Delhi: Concept Publishing, 2002.

Urquhart, D. J. "The Distribution and Use of Scientific and Technical Information." *The Royal Society Scientific Information Conference, June 21–July 2, 1948. Report and Papers Submitted,* 408–19. London: The Royal Society, 1948.

Index

Note: Page numbers followed by *f* indicate pages with figures.

number of items checked out, 85

percentage of items checked out, 85

totaling number of items, 109, 110*f*

SUSHI (Standardized Usage Statistics Harvesting Initiative), 149

symbols, nonnumerical, in Year column, 53, 54*f*

T

text files

converting to Excel files, 43–45

importing into Excel, 37–40

Text Import Wizard, 37–40

time frames, staggered, for borrowing, 124

Titlewise (Follett Company), 47

totaling number of items in summary file, 109, 110*f*. *See also* addition in Excel

turnover. *See* average use per title

.txt files, 37. *See also* text files

type of material, use by, 89

U

unavailable items, 85, 86

uncounted materials, 4–5

Undo command, 78

undoing text, 31, 32*f*

use, definition, 1–2

use costs, analysis by, 145

use studies

advantages and disadvantages, 7–8

further research opportunities, 152–154

research on, 150–152

user-defined functions in Excel, 56, 59*f*

users, analysis of, 146–147

V

Values and Number Formats option, 67

variances, definition, 126

vendor-supplied analysis, 46–47

W

website for this book, vi, 46, 56

weeding

and correlation of age to use, 105

and increases in circulation, 151

and relative use, 118, 122

and use studies, 3

width of column

changing, 15

and number signs (#) in cells, 41

using text wrap, 106

workbooks in Excel, 10

working file

creation of, 48, 62

definition, 33

worksheets in Excel, 10

change name of, 17

creating new worksheets, 89

deleting, 22, 23*f*

inserting new worksheets, 17, 18*f*

Y

Year column. *See* date of publication

Tony Greiner, a librarian at Portland (OR) Community College, works in collection development, reference, and bibliographic instruction. He has contributed to *Library Journal* and *Public Libraries*. Prior to becoming a librarian, he taught school, played the trombone, and drove the hippo truck for Carson and Barnes Circus. He received his MLS from Emporia State University.

Bob Cooper has fourteen years of collection development experience in public and special libraries. He has over ten years of expertise using Microsoft Office products, including Excel. He earned his MLS from the University of Denver.